STANDARD LOAN

The College, Merthyr Tydfil Learning Zone
University of South Wales CF48 1AR
Tel: 01685 726005

Books are to be returned on or before the last date below

2 3 FEB 2015

BENTHYCIAD SAFONOL

Man Dysgu Y Coleg, Merthyr Tudful
Prifysgol De Cymru CF48 1AR
Ffôn: 01685 726005

Rhaid dychwelyd y llyfrau ar neu cy

FOCUS ON SOCIAL WORK LAW
Series Editor: Alison Brammer

Palgrave Macmillan's Focus on Social Work Law series consists of compact, accessible guides to the principles, structures and processes of particular areas of the law as they apply to social work practice. Designed to develop students' understanding as well as refresh practitioners' knowledge, each book provides focused, digestible and navigable content in an easily portable form.

Available now

Looked After Children, Caroline Ball
Child Protection, Kim Holt
Capacity and Autonomy, Robert Johns
Making Good Decisions, Michael Preston-Shoot

Forthcoming titles

Court and Legal Skills, Penny Cooper
Adoption and Permanency, Philip Musson
Youth Justice, Jo Staines
Children in Need of Support, Joanne Westwood
Safeguarding Adults, Alison Brammer

Author of the bestselling textbook *Social Work Law*, Alison Brammer is a qualified solicitor with specialist experience working in Social Services, including child protection, adoption, mental health and community care. Alison coordinates the MA in Child Care Law and Practice and the MA in Adult Safeguarding at Keele University.

Series Standing Order

ISBN 9781137017833 paperback
(*outside North America only*)

You can receive future titles in this series as they are published by placing a standing order. Please contact your bookseller or, in the case of difficulty, write to us at the address below with your name and address, the title of the series and the ISBN quoted above.

Customer Services Department, Macmillan Distribution Ltd
Houndmills, Basingstoke, Hampshire RG21 6XS, England

LOOKED AFTER CHILDREN

CAROLINE BALL

palgrave
macmillan

First published 2014 by
PALGRAVE MACMILLAN

Palgrave Macmillan in the UK is an imprint of Macmillan Publishers
Limited, registered in England, company number 785998, of Houndmills,
Basingstoke, Hampshire RG21 6XS.

Palgrave Macmillan in the US is a division of St Martin's Press LLC,
175 Fifth Avenue, New York, NY 10010.

Palgrave Macmillan is the global academic imprint of the above companies
and has companies and representatives throughout the world.

Palgrave® and Macmillan® are registered trademarks in the United States,
the United Kingdom, Europe and other countries

ISBN: 978–1–137–28651–2

This book is printed on paper suitable for recycling and made from fully
managed and sustained forest sources. Logging, pulping and manufacturing
processes are expected to conform to the environmental regulations of the
country of origin.

A catalogue record for this book is available from the British Library.

A catalog record for this book is available from the Library of Congress.

Typeset by Cambrian Typesetters, Camberley, Surrey

Printed and bound in the UK by The Lavenham Press Ltd, Suffolk

In grateful memory of
John Malcolm Ball
1941–2013

CONTENTS

TABLE OF CASES

TABLE OF LEGISLATION

Regulations

Other

ACKNOWLEDGMENTS

As a lawyer researching and teaching the legal framework of social work practice, I am conscious of the extent to which I have been indebted, over many years, to my academic colleagues in the School of Social Work at the University of East Anglia and to local practitioners for valuable insights into the interface between the law and practice with vulnerable parents and children. Happily, this continues. I am most grateful for the generous sharing of expertise by my former academic colleagues, Dr Beth Neil and Dr Jonathan Dickens, and the practice wisdom in specialist areas of senior social work practitioners and managers Wendy Dyde, Sarah-Jane Smedmor, Sue Gee and Zoë Martin. Their collective contribution has been invaluable in helping a lawyer to appreciate the complexities of applying the law across this multi-layered area of child care practice; any errors are, of course, entirely my own.

ABBREVIATIONS

BAAF	British Association for Adoption and Fostering
CAFCASS	Children and Family Court Advisory and Support Service
CAMHS	Child and Adolescent Mental Health Service
DCSF	Department for Children Schools and Families
DCLG	Department for Communities and Local Government
DfE	Department for Education
DfES	Department for Education and Skills
DH	Department of Health
DHSS	Department of Health and Social Security
EPO	emergency protection order
ECHR	European Convention on Human Rights and Fundamental Freedoms
IRO	independent reviewing officer
LAC review	looked after children review
LASPO	Legal Aid, Sentencing and Punishment of Offenders Act 2012
LGO	local government ombudsman
NAIRO	National Association of Independent Reviewing Officers
NCB	National Children's Bureau
NMS	National Minimum Standards
NSPCC	National Society for the Prevention of Cruelty to Children
Ofsted	Office for Standards in Education, Children's Services and Skills
PACE	Police and Criminal Evidence Act 1984
UKBA	UK Border Agency
UASC	Unaccompanied asylum-seeking children
UNCRC	United Nations Committee on the Rights of the Child

USING THIS BOOK

Aim of the series

Welcome to the Focus on Social Work Law Series.

This introductory section aims to elucidate the aims and philosophy of the series; introduce some key themes that run through the series; outline the key features within each volume; and offer a brief legal skills guide to complement use of the series.

The Social Work Law Focus Series provides a distinct range of specialist resources for students and practitioners. Each volume provides an accessible and practical discussion of the law applicable to a particular area of practice. The length of each volume ensures that whilst portable and focused there is nevertheless a depth of coverage of each topic beyond that typically contained in comprehensive textbooks addressing all aspects of social work law and practice.

Each volume includes the relevant principles, structures and processes of the law (with case law integrated into the text) and highlights clearly the application of the law to practice. A key objective for each text is to identify the policy context of each area of practice and the factors that have shaped the law into its current presentation. As law is constantly developing and evolving, where known, likely future reform of the law is identified. Each book takes a critical approach, noting inconsistencies, omissions and other challenges faced by those charged with its implementation.

The significance of the Human Rights Act 1998 to social work practice is a common theme in each text and implications of the Act for practice in the particular area are identified with inclusion of relevant case law.

The series focuses on the law in England and Wales. Some references may be made to comparable aspects of law in Scotland and Northern Ireland, particularly to highlight differences in approach. With devolution in Scotland and the expanding role of the Welsh Assembly Government it will be important for practitioners in those areas and working at the borders to be familiar with any such differences.

Features

At a glance content lists

Each chapter begins with a bullet point list summarizing the key points within the topic included in that chapter. From this list the reader can see 'at a glance' how the materials are organized and what to expect in that section. The introductory chapter provides an overview of the book, outlining coverage in each chapter that enables the reader to see how the topic develops throughout the text. The boundaries of the discussion are set including, where relevant, explicit recognition of areas that are excluded from the text.

Key case analysis

One of the key aims of the series is to emphasize an integrated understanding of law, comprising legislation and case law and practice. For this reason each chapter includes at least one key case analysis feature focusing on a particularly significant case. The facts of the case are outlined in brief followed by analysis of the implications of the decision for social work practice in a short commentary. Given the significance of the selected cases, readers are encouraged to follow up references and read the case in full together with any published commentaries.

On-the-spot questions

These questions are designed to consolidate learning and prompt reflection on the material considered. These questions may be used as a basis for discussion with colleagues or fellow students and may also prompt consideration or further investigation of how the law is applied within a particular setting or authority, for example, looking at information provided to service users on a council website. Questions may also follow key cases, discussion of research findings or practice scenarios, focusing on the issues raised and application of the relevant law to practice.

Practice focus

Each volume incorporates practice-focused case scenarios to demonstrate how the law is applied to social work practice. The scenarios may be fictional or based on an actual decision.

Further reading

Each chapter closes with suggestions for further reading to develop knowledge and critical understanding. Annotated to explain the reasons for inclusion, the reader may be directed to classic influential pieces, such as enquiry reports, up-to-date research and analysis of issues discussed in the chapter, and relevant policy documents. In addition students may wish to read in full the case law included throughout the text and to follow up references integrated into discussion of each topic.

Websites

As further important sources of information, websites are also included in the text with links from the companion website. Some may be a gateway to access significant documents including government publications, others may provide accessible information for service users or present a particular perspective on an area, such as the voices of experts by experience. Given the rapid development of law and practice across the range of topics covered in the series, reference to relevant websites can be a useful way to keep pace with actual and anticipated changes

Glossary

Each text includes a subject-specific glossary of key terms for quick reference and clarification. A flashcard version of the glossary is available on the companion website.

Visual aids

As appropriate, visual aids are included where information may be presented accessibly as a table, graph or flow chart. This approach is particularly helpful for the presentation of some complex areas of law and to demonstrate structured decision-making or options available.

Companion site

The series-wide companion site www.palgrave.com/socialworklaw provides additional learning resources, including flashcard glossaries, web links, a legal skills guide, and a blog to communicate important developments and updates. The site will also host a student feedback zone.

Key sources of law

In this section an outline of the key sources of law considered through-out the series is provided. The following 'Legal skills' section includes some guidance on the easiest ways to access and understand these sources.

Legislation

The term legislation is used interchangeably with Acts of Parliament and statutes to refer to primary sources of law.

All primary legislation is produced through the parliamentary process, beginning its passage as a Bill. Bills may have their origins as an expressed policy in a government manifesto, in the work of the Law Commission, or following and responding to a significant event such as a child death or the work of a government department such as the Home Office.

Each Bill is considered by both the House of Lords and House of Commons, debated and scrutinized through various committee stages before becoming an Act on receipt of royal assent.

Legislation has a title and year, for example, the Equality Act 2010. Legislation can vary in length from an Act with just one section to others with over a hundred. Lengthy Acts are usually divided into headed 'Parts' (like chapters) containing sections, subsections and paragraphs. For example, s. 31 of the Children Act 1989 is in Part IV entitled 'Care and Supervision' and outlines the criteria for care order applications. Beyond the main body of the Act the legislation may also include 'Schedules' following the main provisions. Schedules have the same force of law as the rest of the Act but are typically used to cover detail such as a list of legislation which has been amended or revoked by the current Act or detailed matters linked to a specific provision, for instance, Schedule 2 of the Children Act 1989 details specific services (e.g. day centres) which may be provided under the duty to safeguard and promote the welfare of children in need, contained in s. 17.

Remember also that statutes often contain sections dealing with inter-pretation or definitions and, although often situated towards the end of the Act, these can be a useful starting point.

Legislation also includes Statutory Instruments which may be in the form of rules, regulations and orders. The term delegated legislation collectively describes this body of law as it is made under delegated authority of Parliament, usually by a minister or government department. Statutory Instruments tend to provide additional detail to the outline scheme provided by the primary legislation, the Act of Parliament. Statutory Instruments are usually cited by year and a number, for example, Local Authority Social Services (Complaints Procedure) Order SI 2006/1681.

Various documents may be issued to further assist with the implementation of legislation including guidance and codes of practice.

Guidance

Guidance documents may be described as formal or practice guidance. Formal guidance may be identified as such where it is stated to have been issued under s. 7(1) of the Local Authority Social Services Act 1970, which provides that 'local authorities shall act under the general guidance of the Secretary of State'. An example of s. 7 guidance is *Working Together to Safeguard Children* (2013, London: Department of Health). The significance of s. 7 guidance was explained by Sedley J in *R v London Borough of Islington, ex parte Rixon* [1997] ELR 66: 'Parliament in enacting s. 7(1) did not intend local authorities to whom ministerial guidance was given to be free, having considered it, to take it or leave it … in my view parliament by s. 7(1) has required local authorities to follow the path charted by the Secretary of State's guidance, with liberty to deviate from it where the local authority judges on admissible grounds that there is good reason to do so, but without freedom to take a substantially different course.' (71)

Practice guidance does not carry s. 7 status but should nevertheless normally be followed as setting examples of what good practice might look like.

Codes of practice

Codes of practice have been issued to support the Mental Health Act 1983 and the Mental Capacity Act 2005. Again, it is a matter of good practice to follow the recommendations of the codes and these lengthy documents include detailed and illustrative scenarios to assist with interpretation and application of the legislation. There may also be a duty on specific people charged with responsibilities under the primary legislation to have regard to the code.

Guidance and codes of practice are available on relevant websites, for example, the Department of Health, as referenced in individual volumes.

Case law

Case law provides a further major source of law. In determining disputes in court the judiciary applies legislation. Where provisions within legislation are unclear or ambiguous the judiciary follows principles of statutory interpretation but at times judges are quite creative.

Some areas of law are exclusively contained in case law and described as common law. Most law of relevance to social work practice is of relatively recent origin and has its primary basis in legislation. Case law remains relevant as it links directly to such legislation and may clarify and explain provisions and terminology within the legislation. The significance of a particular decision will depend on the position of the court in a hierarchy whereby the Supreme Court is most senior and the magistrates' court is junior. Decisions of the higher courts bind the lower courts – they must be followed. This principle is known as the doctrine of precedent. Much legal debate takes place as to the precise element of a ruling which subsequently binds other decisions. This is especially the case where in the Court of Appeal or Supreme Court there are between three and five judges hearing a case, majority judgments are allowed and different judges may arrive at the same conclusion but for different reasons. Where a judge does not agree with the majority, the term dissenting judgment is applied.

It is important to understand how cases reach court. Many cases in social work law are based on challenges to the way a local authority has exercised its powers. This is an aspect of administrative law known as judicial review where the central issue for the court is not the substance of the decision taken by the authority but the way it was taken. Important considerations will be whether the authority has exceeded its powers, failed to follow established procedures or acted irrationally.

Before an individual can challenge an authority in judicial review it will usually be necessary to exhaust other remedies first, including local authority complaints procedures. If unsatisfied with the outcome of a complaint an individual has a further option which is to complain to the local government ombudsman (LGO). The LGO investigates alleged cases of maladministration and may make recommendations to local authorities including the payment of financial compensation. Ombudsman decisions may be accessed on the LGO website and make interesting reading. In cases involving social services, a common concern across children's and adults' services is unreasonable delay in carrying out assessments and providing services. See www.lgo.org.uk.

Classification of law

The above discussion related to the sources and status of laws. It is also important to note that law can serve a variety of functions and may be grouped into recognized classifications. For law relating to social work practice key classifications distinguish between law which is criminal or civil and law which is public or private.

Whilst acknowledging the importance of these classifications, it must also be appreciated that individual concerns and circumstances may not always fall so neatly into the same categories, a given scenario may engage with criminal, civil, public and private law.

- Criminal law relates to alleged behaviour which is defined by statute or common law as an offence prosecuted by the state, carrying a penalty which may include imprisonment. The offence must be proved 'beyond reasonable doubt'.
- Civil law is the term applied to all other areas of law and often focuses on disputes between individuals. A lower standard of proof, 'balance of probabilities', applies in civil cases.
- Public law is that in which society has some interest and involves a public authority, such as care proceedings.
- Private law operates between individuals, such as marriage or contract.

Legal skills guide: accessing and understanding the law

Legislation

Legislation may be accessed as printed copies published by The Stationery Office and is also available online. Some books on a particular area of law will include a copy of the Act (sometimes annotated) and this is a useful way of learning about new laws. As time goes by, however, and amendments are made to legislation it can become increasingly difficult to keep track of the up-to-date version of an Act. Revised and up-to-date versions of legislation (as well as the version originally enacted) are available on the website www.legislation.gov.uk.

Legislation may also be accessed on the Parliament website. Here, it is possible to trace the progress of current and draft Bills and a link to Hansard provides transcripts of debates on Bills as they pass through both Houses of Parliament, www.parliament.uk.

Bills and new legislation are often accompanied by 'Explanatory notes' which can give some background to the development of the new law and offer useful explanations of each provision.

Case law

Important cases are reported in law reports available in traditional bound volumes (according to court, specialist area or general weekly reports) or online. Case referencing is known as citation and follows particular conventions according to whether a hard copy law report or online version is sought.

Citation of cases in law reports begins with the names of the parties, followed by the year and volume number of the law report, followed by an abbreviation of the law report title, then the page number. For example: *Lawrence v Pembrokeshire CC* [2007] 2 FLR 705. The case is reported in volume 2 of the 2007 Family Law Report at page 705.

Online citation, sometimes referred to as neutral citation because it is not linked to a particular law report, also starts with the names of the parties, followed by the year in which the case was decided, followed by an abbreviation of the court in which the case was heard, followed by a number representing the place in the order of cases decided by that court. For example: *R (Macdonald) v Royal Borough of Kensington and Chelsea* [2011] UKSC 33. Neutral citation of this case shows that it was a 2011 decision of the Supreme Court.

University libraries tend to have subscriptions to particular legal databases, such as 'Westlaw', which can be accessed by those enrolled as students, often via direct links from the university library webpage. Westlaw and LexisNexis are especially useful as sources of case law, statutes and other legal materials. Libraries usually have their own guides to these sources, again often published on their websites. For most cases there is a short summary or analysis as well as the full transcript.

As not everyone using the series will be enrolled at a university, the following website can be accessed without any subscription: BAILLI (British and Irish Legal Information Institute) www.bailii.org. This site includes judgments from the full range of UK court services including the Supreme Court, Court of Appeal and High Court but also features a wide range of tribunal decisions. Judgments for Scotland, Northern Ireland and the Republic of Ireland are also available as are judgments of the European Court of Human Rights.

Whether accessed via a law report or online, the presentation of cases follows a template. The report begins with the names of the parties, the court which heard the cases, names(s) of the judges(s) and dates of the hearing. This is followed by a summary of key legal issues involved in the case (often in italics) known as catchwords, then the headnote, which is a paragraph or so stating the key facts of the case and the nature of the claim or dispute or the criminal charge. 'HELD' indicates the ruling of the court. This is followed by a list of cases that were referred to in legal argument during the hearing, a summary of the journey of the case through appeal processes, names of the advocates and then the start of the full judgment(s) given by the judge(s). The judgment usually recounts the circumstances of the case, findings of fact and findings on the law and reasons for the decision.

If stuck on citations the Cardiff Index to Legal Abbreviations is a useful resource at www.legalabbrevs.cardiff.ac.uk.

There are numerous specific guides to legal research providing more detailed examination of legal materials but the best advice on developing legal skills is to start exploring the above and to read some case law – it's surprisingly addictive!

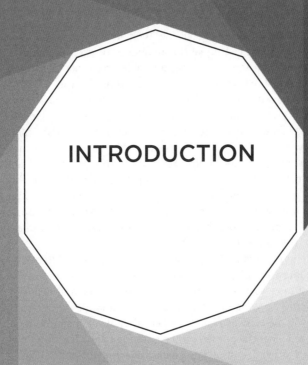

INTRODUCTION

AT A GLANCE THIS CHAPTER COVERS:

- an historical overview of child care policy and legislation in the twentieth and early twenty-first centuries
- the development of the policy context in which the current law operates
- an outline of the topics included
- Human Rights Act 1998 issues
- challenges of this practice area

Historical overview

From Poor Law to welfare

The state's care of children outside their families changed radically during the twentieth century and continues to develop. In the previous century, apart from some boarding-out initiatives, organized by philanthropic individuals within the Poor Law provisions (George, 1970, ch. 1), little attention was paid to the welfare of the orphaned or abandoned **child**. After years of failed campaigns, in response to the deaths of numerous children looked after for reward by so-called 'baby farmers', the first law regulating the care of children, the Infant Life Protection Act 1872, reached the statute book. Several statutory provisions followed, but none proved effective in terms of improving the lot of the children involved, least of all, under the Prevention of Cruelty to Children Act 1889, the transfer to the Poor Law guardians of **parental responsibility** for children removed from their parents on the grounds of mistreatment or neglect (Hendrick, 1994, ch. 2).

Despite its designation as a 'children's charter', the Children Act 1908 did not address the plight of children in the public care. For most of the first half of the twentieth century, the majority of children deprived of a normal home life were maintained by local authorities under Poor Law provisions as persons in need of relief. They were therefore regarded primarily as a financial burden on their communities. The final Poor Law Act, passed in 1930, consolidated earlier enactments for the relief of the poor and was administered by local authorities, generally acting through public assistance committees. The duty of the local authority in regard to children 'To set to work or put out as apprentices all children whose parents are not, in the opinion of the Council, able to keep and maintain their children' (s. 15) starkly reflected the overall imperative – to reduce the burden on rate payers rather than any consideration for children's welfare.

After the 1939–1945 war, starting with the Children Act 1948, **legislation** (informed by a burgeoning interest in children's welfare and professionalization of child care) increasingly recognized the state's responsibility for the welfare of children and placed a growing body of duties on local authorities to fulfil that responsibility. Symbolically, this is reflected in s. 12(1) Children Act 1948, which, in contrast to the Poor Law duty, required local authorities, through their newly established Children's Committees: 'to exercise their powers with respect to [the child] so as to further his best interests, and to afford him opportunity for the proper development of his character and abilities'.

This chapter seeks to set the current law, addressed under discrete topics in the rest of the text, in its historical and policy context by exploring two key themes or policy drivers that have emerged from the 1940s until the present day. These are identified as:

- the growth in local authorities' powers and duties to safeguard the welfare of looked after children, now acknowledged in the concept of corporate parenthood; and
- an increasing raft of measures aimed at reducing the gap in lifelong outcomes between children brought up in the public care and the rest of the population.

The chapter concludes with reflection as to the extent to which it is realistic to expect local authorities to properly fulfil these responsibilities within a climate of increased demand and constrained resources.

Growth in local authorities' powers and duties

Post-war reforms

Under the Poor Law provisions administered by public assistance authorities, children could be placed in a wide range of institutions, including many run by voluntary organizations. Certain children, initially orphans and deserted children and those over whom the local authority had assumed parental rights, could also be boarded out in foster homes. During and after the Second World War (1939–1945), the rules regarding eligibility for boarding-out were relaxed and finally abolished. The whole system for placing children away from their homes was one of infinite complexity, involving three government departments and a confusing web of local statutory and voluntary committees. The public outcry that followed the death of Dennis O'Neill at the hands of his foster parents in January 1945 and the publication of the inquiry which followed (Monkton, 1945) together with the campaigning of Lady Allen of Hurtwood and others, exemplified in a letter to *The Times* (5 July 1944), led to the setting up of the interdepartmental Care of Children Committee, chaired by Dame Myra Curtis. Its terms of reference were:

> To inquire into existing methods of providing for children who from loss
> of parents or from any other cause whatever are deprived of a normal
> home life with their own parents or **relatives**; and to consider what
> further measures should be taken to ensure that these children are
> brought up under conditions best calculated to compensate them for
> the lack of parental care.
>
> *Ministry of Health and Ministry of Education, 1946*

At the time the Curtis Committee was gathering its evidence, 85 per cent
of children maintained by public assistance authorities were placed in
children's homes, voluntary homes and hospitals (Ministry of Health and
Ministry of Education, 1946, table 1). The members of the Curtis
Committee worked incredibly hard. They made a large number of mostly
unannounced visits to observe conditions in all types of institutions and
foster homes across England and Wales, as well as minutely analysing the
ways in which the system was administered. The committee's report
describes, in measured but graphic terms, observation of 'a picture of
administrative chaos and human suffering' (Griffith, 1966, p. 361). In
particular, it identified:

- the overlapping responsibilities of several government departments
  devolved to a confused network of local committees;
- high numbers of children poorly cared for in low-quality, impersonal,
  institutions;
- a serious lack of child care expertise among those working with children.

The committee was, bravely considering the O'Neill case, clear that, as
had been advocated by the Mundella Committee 50 years earlier
(George, 1970), the placement of choice should be **foster care** and, for
those with no hope of returning to their families, adoption. Based on the
evidence from its thorough review, the Curtis Committee made robust
recommendations. For the first time the focus was to be on the welfare
of the individual child instead of the bleak duty in the Poor Law Act 1930,
referred to above. Other recommendations included:

- a single department of state, the Home Office, to have overall responsibility for children cared for away from their homes;
- local authorities to appoint dedicated Children's Committees employ-
  ing experienced and suitably qualified children's officers to exercise
  statutory powers and duties in regard to children in their area;

- a determined drive to recruit more foster parents, with the aim of ultimately phasing out institutional care; and
- inspections of all foster homes and institutions.

Most of the Curtis Committee's recommendations were enacted in the
Children Act 1948. Within a relatively short time after the Act came into
force, the pressure to move children from institutions into foster care,
governed by Boarding Out Regulations made under the Act, resulted in
a significant increase in the use of foster care (Packman, 1975). Over the
next 40 years, a sequence of child care-related legislation impacted on
the regulation of all aspects of child care and protection, including
fostering.

Local authorities' powers and responsibilities, 1963–1989

The Curtis Committee identified local authority provision of supportive
services to prevent the need for children to be removed from their
homes as an essential responsibility. Unfortunately, its terms of reference
precluded the committee making recommendations to that effect. This
was recognized as a significant gap in the reforms introduced by the
Children Act 1948 and a sustained campaign for preventative powers
ensued (Packman, 1975, ch. 4). Eventually the deficit was remedied
when the terms of reference for a Home Office committee under the
chairmanship of Lord Ingleby, set up in 1956, included the direction to
'inquire into and make recommendations' on:

> Whether local authorities should ... be given new powers and
> duties to prevent or forestall the suffering of children through
> neglect in their own homes. (Home Office, 1960: para. 1)

The Committee's recommendations were enacted in s. 1 Children and
Young Persons Act 1963:

> It shall be the duty of every local authority to make available such
> advice, guidance and assistance as may promote the welfare of children
> by diminishing the need to receive children into or keep them in care.

This power, very much amplified, has its current manifestation in Part III
Children Act 1989.

The Local Authority Social Services Act 1970, which came into force
prior to the partial implementation of the Children and Young Persons
Act 1969, effected the complete reorganization of local authority social

services into generic social work departments, resulting in the loss of much of the social work child care expertise built up in local authority children departments since the 1948 Act (Packman, 1975, ch. 8). The next decade saw frenetic legislative activity: the Children Act 1975, Adoption Act 1976 and Foster Children Act 1980, the combined effect being twofold. Local authorities' responsibilities and discretion as to how their powers were exercised were substantially increased (Packman et al., 1986; Ball, 1998) and, because of the piecemeal amendment of existing legislation, child care law, already complex, became tortuously so.

By the early 1980s the state of public child law was seen to be frustrating rather than helping good child care practice. In the words of a group of lawyers and social workers giving evidence to the House of Commons Social Services Committee, which had chosen for its 1982/1983 session the topic of 'children in care':

> The present state of children's legislation can only be described as complex, confusing and unsatisfactory ... The effect and implication of this on children is diverse with far-reaching consequences for their welfare. (House of Commons, 1984:118)

The consequences were only too clearly demonstrated by the findings of a substantial body of government-funded research into all aspects of social work decision-making within the existing statutory framework (DHSS, 1985). The poor practice identified in these studies included:

- defensive, ill-planned crisis interventions in families already well known to social services departments, with overuse of statutory provisions rather than voluntary care (Packman et al., 1986); and
- the lack of active work to maintain links between children in care and their birth families, resulting in lengthy care episodes and many children losing all contact with their families (Millham et al., 1986) (see below, page 65).

The separate reform processes in relation to the **public law** and **private law** which culminated in the Children Act 1989 have been well documented (see, for example, Ball, 1990; Masson, 2000; White et al., 2008: ch. 1). The 1989 Act, described by the Lord Chancellor, Lord MacKay, as 'the most comprehensive and far-reaching reform of child law which has come before Parliament in living memory' (HL Deb 1988, vol. 502, col. 488), came into force in 1991. It transformed public and private child law with shared concepts and a single set of principles, administered in a relatively coherent court structure. The public law cornerstone of the 1989 Act, Part III, which builds on the preventative duty first introduced in 1963, provides for services for children in need, including accommodation of the child, in partnership with families. Parts IV and V provide for court orders and powers to intervene to protect children from significant harm. Although the legal differentiation between public and private law proceedings is clear, Bainham (2013) suggests that in practice many cases are hybrid, containing elements of both public and private law.

The policy context of current legislation and guidance

Many of the post-1991 amendments to Part III reflect a growing recognition of the extent to which children growing up for most or part of their childhood as looked after children in the public care, whether under care orders (Part IV) or on a voluntary basis under Part III, suffer lifelong social and educational disadvantage. In 1998, in response to Sir William Utting's penetrating critique of the care system (Utting, 1997), the government launched its Quality Protects programme as part of a range of initiatives to tackle social exclusion and childhood poverty. The Quality Protects programme, initially scheduled for three years but extended to 2004, linked funding to targets for local authorities to improve outcomes for looked after children in areas such as placement stability and educational attainment (Chase et al., 2006). Nine linked research studies were commissioned as part of the programme (Stein, 2009a).

The death of Victoria Climbié and the introduction of the Every Child Matters agenda

In 2000, Victoria, aged eight, was murdered by her great aunt (by whom she was privately fostered) and her partner. The circumstances surrounding the ill-treatment and death of Victoria and the failure of many involved agencies to protect her were the subject of intense media interest and public outrage. A review into the circumstances surrounding her death, chaired by Lord Laming, followed (2003). Alongside a detailed response to Lord Laming's report, and a report produced by the Social Exclusion Unit (2003) on raising the educational attainment of children in care, the government published the Green Paper *Every Child Matters* (Chief Secretary to the Treasury, 2003) setting out an aspirational agenda to reform and improve the care of all children.

Following detailed consultation, many of the proposals in the Green Paper were enacted in the Children Act 2004, which, as well as many other reforms, including making directors of children's services and lead members directly accountable for children's social care and education, amended the Children Act 1989 to place a new duty on local authorities to promote the educational achievement of looked after children (s. 22(3A)).

Additional support for looked after children

The 2004 Act provided the statutory framework for implementation of the Every Child Matters agenda to improve outcomes with regard to health, staying safe, enjoying and achieving, making a positive contribution and achieving economic well-being for all children. However, when compared to all children, lifelong outcomes for looked after children were recognized to be very poor and in need of further statutory support (DfES, 2006). The Children and Young Persons Act 2008 enacted those proposals in the White Paper *Care Matters: Time for Change* which required legislation (DfES, 2007).

Implementation of many of the White Paper proposals was achievable through revision of regulations and statutory guidance rather than primary legislation. This resulted in a raft of new regulations and guidance documents, impacting on all aspects of the care of looked after children, which came into force in 2011 and will be referred to throughout this volume.

The Children and Families Act 2014

The Act enacts a range of government commitments which are aimed at improving services for children in the adoption and care systems, those affected by decisions of the family courts and those with special educational needs. The reforms are noted throughout this text, though at present there is no indication as to when they may be implemented.

Topics included

This book aims to provide its readers with an understanding of the law relating to looked after children which has not before been brought together in this way. Following this introductory chapter, Chapter 1 provides an overview of current legislation and guidance and reference to key research, much more of which is referred to in subsequent chapters.

Chapter 2 examines accommodation under s. 20 Children Act 1989; and Chapter 3 alternative routes to the looked after status. The following three chapters cover local authorities' responsibilities to looked after children: Chapter 4 examines the responsibilities of the local authority as corporate parent in terms of assessment and planning; Chapter 5 addresses the voice of the looked after child and the role of the family in decision-making as well as contact and accountability issues; and the focus of Chapter 6 is on the range of placement options for looked after children. Chapter 7 covers reviews and the role of the independent reviewing officer (IRO), and Chapter 8 alternative legal arrangements. Finally, Chapter 9 addresses local authorities' responsibilities towards care leavers.

On-the-spot questions

1 What are the most significant child care-related legislative milestones of the twentieth and twenty-first centuries?
2 Which of these focus on the particular needs of looked after children?

The European Convention on Human Rights and the Human Rights Act 1998

The European Convention on Human Rights and Fundamental Freedoms (ECHR) was designed to protect all humans at a time before the concept of children having rights received international attention. However, children are persons entitled to claim its protection.

For very many years before the Human Rights Act 1998 came in to force, actions in the European Court of Human Rights against the UK for breaches of the ECHR led to significant piecemeal reforms of several areas of public child law. These included: an end to the administrative procedure whereby local authorities could assume parental rights over children they were looking after, and the provision of limited rights to parents in regard to contact with children in care. The Children Act 1989 was drafted with greater awareness of the need for compliance with the ECHR than previous child care legislation.

The Human Rights Act 1998, which allows individuals to challenge public bodies' actions as being incompatible with Convention rights, came into force in 2000 and has had a profound impact on family law. However, Jane Fortin's powerful critique of judicial failure to separate the rights of children from those of their parents suggests that in many public and private law cases children's rights may still not be given sufficient attention (Fortin, 2011). In regard to looked after children, the key ECHR articles are Articles 3, 6, 8 and, in conjunction with any of these, 14.

Article 3: the unqualified right not to be subjected to torture or to inhuman or degrading treatment

In terms of social work practice with looked after children, had the 1998 Act been in force when the 'pin-down' regime was being endured by children in Staffordshire (Levy and Kahan, 1991), it would have been open to challenge as being in breach of Article 3, as would any similar disproportionate restraint practice. It has also been invoked where a local authority failed to protect children from abuse (*Z v UK* [2001]) and to challenge the defence of 'reasonable chastisement' of a child where the punishment caused actual bodily harm (*A v UK (Human Rights: Punishment of Child)* [1998]).

Article 5: the right to liberty and security of person

Article 5 is qualified by a list of exceptions which include: '(d) the detention of a minor by lawful order for the purposes of educational supervision or his lawful detention for the purposes of bringing him before the competent legal authority'.

Prior to implementation of the 1998 Act, there was speculation that the **secure accommodation** provisions under the Children Act 1989 (see pages 89–90) might breach Article 5. The Court of Appeal in *Re K (A Child) (Secure Accommodation Order: Right to Liberty)* [2001], a case heard shortly after implementation of the 1998 Act, refused to find any breach, holding that the detention of a child in secure accommodation, following the criteria in s. 25 Children Act 1989 and the requirements in the Children (Secure Accommodation) Regulations 1991, came within the Article 5(d) exception.

Article 6: the right to a fair trial

> In the determination of his civil rights and obligations ... everyone is entitled to a fair and public hearing ... by an impartial tribunal established by law. Judgment shall be pronounced publicly but the press and public may be excluded from all or part of the trial in the interest of morals, public order or national security in a democratic society, where the interests of

juveniles or the protection of the private life of the parties so require, or to the extent necessary in the opinion of the court in special circumstances where publicity would prejudice the interests of justice.

Article 6 ECHR

Article 6, together with Article 8, provides procedural rights for family members involved in disputes with the state in child protection and adoption proceedings as well as disputes between private individuals.

Article 8

(1) Everyone has the right to respect for his private and family life, his home and his correspondence.
(2) There shall be no interference by a public authority with the exercise of this right except such as is in accordance with the law and is necessary in a democratic society in the interests of national security, public safety or the economic well-being of the country, for the prevention of disorder or crime, for the protection of health or morals, or for the protection of the rights and freedoms of others.

Article 8 ECHR

Whilst it is hard to envisage a greater infringement of the family life of parents than when a care order is made, except for adoption of their child against their wishes, both, provided due process is followed, come within the qualification of being in accordance with law and necessary in a democratic society for 'the protection of the rights and freedom of others', namely the child.

Article 14

The enjoyment of the rights and freedoms set forth in this Convention shall be secured without discrimination on any ground such as sex, race, colour, language, religion, political or other opinion, national or social origin, association with a national minority, property, birth or other status.

Article 14 ECHR

It should be noted that Article 14 only prohibits discrimination in the enjoyment of rights guaranteed under the ECHR, not all discrimination.

It also has to be shown that it is persons in relatively similar situations who are being treated differently (*Burden v UK* [2008])

> **On-the-spot question**   How has the Human Rights Act 1998 increased the impact of the ECHR on domestic decision-making?

Challenges of this practice area

Working on this book, it has become apparent that the author's struggle to address such a multi-layered topic in a coherent way reflects the reality of social work with looked after children: work that is both highly regulated and dependent, in terms of successful outcomes for the children involved, on dedicated, high quality, time-consuming practice. Faced on the one hand with statutory guidance setting out properly high expectations in regard to quality social work and multi-agency practice with looked after children, and on the other with diminishing resources and externally imposed performance targets, there have to be concerns as to whether, confronted with increasing demand, the former can be delivered within the constraints of the latter.

Well before the swingeing resource reductions of recent years, MacDonald (2009) published an impassioned critique of successive governments' policies and legislation. He suggested that: 'Government understands well the value of the care system to those it is designed to protect, as well as the value of that system to society as a whole.'

The problem he identifies is that: 'when it is looked at in the broader context of the parlous state of human, structural and financial resourcing within the care system, the Government's understanding of its worth begins to look increasingly superficial' (at 30).

The issue of resource constraint and the demands of meeting performance targets, preventing delivery of the quality of service expected, will be only too familiar to frontline workers and their managers. At particular points in the chapters that follow, this is demonstrated by conflicting policies, research findings and judicial or academic comment.

Recent policy developments in regard to early intervention, based on the recommendations made by Professor Eileen Munro in her *Review of Child Protection* (Department for Education, 2011c), tackle resource constraints from a different angle. Whilst recognizing the reality of diminished resources, Munro argued that a more highly skilled social work workforce working with their statutory partners to secure provision of early help to families, before problems develop or when they are at a low level, is not only morally right, it is also cost-effective (at 5.9–10). She does not, however, underestimate the dangers of significant concurrent restructuring in all major partner agencies having the potential to disrupt integrated professional provision of early help (5.24–28). Many of Munro's recommendations have been incorporated in the 2013 version of the statutory guidance *Working Together to Safeguard Children* (HM Government, 2013).

Further reading

Department for Education and Skills (2006) *Care Matters: Transforming the Lives of Children and Young People in Care*. The introductory chapter of this Green Paper provides the policy context for the reforms enacted by the Children and Young Persons Act 2008 and amplified in updated regulations and statutory guidance.

Masson, J (2000) 'From Curtis to Waterhouse: state care and child protection in the UK 1945–2000' in Sandford et al. (eds), *Cross Currents: Family Law and Policy in the US and England*. This chapter provides an excellent overview of the development of child care policy and legislation over the second half of the twentieth century.

Probert, R (2012) *Cretney and Probert's Family Law*. Chapter 1, paras 1–021 to 1–033, provides a clear and accessible account of relevant articles of the ECHR and the way in which the Human Rights Act 1998 increases their impact on domestic social work practice.

1

OVERVIEW OF LEGISLATION, GUIDANCE AND KEY RESEARCH

AT A GLANCE THIS CHAPTER COVERS:

- the accompanying statutory and practice guidance
- key themes and issues addressed by leading researchers in the field

Overview of legislation and guidance

Children may become 'looked after':

- as part of a child in need plan for their care, with the consent of, or no objections from, those with parental responsibility; or
- in any circumstances where there is no one to look after a child in need;
- when made the subject of a care order or interim care order in **care proceedings** and placed away from home; or
- for a shorter time as a result of an emergency by means of a child protection order, police protection or detention; or
- when in police custody, on remand or subject to a court order with a residence requirement in criminal proceedings.

All these routes are statutorily defined within the Children Act 1989, Parts III, IV and V and accompanying regulations and guidance.

Since its implementation in 1991, the primary act, the Children Act 1989, has been much amended by: the Children (Leaving Care Act) 2000, the Care Standards Act 2000, the Adoption and Children Act 2002, the Children Act 2004, the Children and Adoption Act 2006, the Children and Young Persons Act 2008, and will be further amended when the Children and Families Act 2014 is implemented. In addition to significantly varying many provisions, the amendments have considerably increased local authorities' responsibilities in regard to the placement of looked after children, the introduction of an independent reviewing service, and the duties owed by local authorities to those formerly looked after. Regulations made under the 1989 Act have been similarly revised. Most of the accompanying combined volumes of regulations and statutory guidance, originally published in 1991 to coincide with implementation of the 1989 Act, were substantially revised and reissued between 2008 and 2011, and further planned revisions are referred to as appropriate. Practitioners need to ensure that the provisions of the primary statute and accompanying regulations and guidance that they consult are those currently in force.

Legislation

Whilst this book is mainly concerned with children looked after by the local authority, and therefore with Parts III, IV and V of the 1989 Act, the possible alternatives to local authority provision of accommodation in

Part II need to be understood and are examined in Chapter 8. The key provisions of the 1989 Act relevant to local authorities' powers and duties in regard to looked after children are contained in the following Parts and accompanying regulations:

- Part III Local Authority Support for Children and Families
- Part IV Care and Supervision
- Part V Protection of Children
- Part VI Community Homes
- Part VII Voluntary Homes and Voluntary Organizations
- Part VIII Registered Children's Homes
- Part IX Private Arrangements for Fostering Children

A key principle underpinning the 1989 Act is that, wherever possible, services to promote and safeguard the welfare of children should be provided in partnership with the child's family. Part III enacts this principle by defining qualification criteria and the range of services to be provided:

(1) It shall be the general duty of every local authority (in addition to the other duties imposed on them by this Part)—
    (a) to safeguard and promote the welfare of children within their area who are in need; and
    (b) so far as is consistent with that duty, to promote the upbringing of such children by their families,
    by providing a range and level of services appropriate to those children's needs.

s. 17 Children Act 1989

Children 'in need' are defined in sub-ss (10) and (11):

(10) For the purposes of this Part a child shall be taken to be in need if—
    (a) he is unlikely to achieve or maintain, or to have the opportunity of achieving or maintaining, a reasonable standard of health or development without the provision for him of services by a local authority under this Part;
    (b) his health or development is likely to be significantly impaired, or further impaired, without the provision for him of such services; or
    (c) he is disabled,
    and 'family', in relation to such a child, includes any person who has parental responsibility for the child and any other person with whom he has been living.

MERTHYR LOANS

MAXIMUM RENEWAL PERIODS

1 WEEK LOAN 10 WEEKS

4 WEEK LOAN 16 WEEKS

HIGH DEMAND 1 WEEK

PLEASE MONITOR YOUR

EMAILS CAREFULLY FOR

ANY RECALLS ON YOUR

BOOKS, FINES WILL BE

CHARGED FOR LATE RETURNS.

(11) For the purposes of this Part, a child is disabled if he is blind, deaf or dumb or suffers from mental disorder of any kind or is substantially and permanently handicapped by illness, injury or congenital deformity or such other disability as may be prescribed; and in this Part—

> 'development' means physical, intellectual, emotional, social or behavioural development;
>
> and 'health' means physical or mental health.

s. 17 Children Act 1989

Children in need are the subject of a separate title in this series (Westwood, 2014). The full range of services which may be provided under Part III, details relating to them, and provisions regarding liability to contribute to the maintenance of looked after children are set out in Schedule 2 to the 1989 Act.

The duty of the local authority in regard to the provision of accommodation for children in need is set out in s. 20 and for children subject to emergency protection orders, in police protection or detention or on remand in s. 21. Its general duties towards looked after children are set out in s. 22, and elaborated in ss 22A–G (which replace the original s. 23). Sections 23ZA and ZB make provision for children in accommodation to be visited and ss 23D–E, 24 and 24A–D set out local authorities' duties towards children previously looked after as they move to adulthood. The stringent criteria regulating the placement of looked after children in secure accommodation are set out in s. 25, and requirements relating to the functions of IROs in ss 25A–C. Detailed provisions regarding the implementation of the duties and responsibilities set out in the primary legislation are to be found in the raft of accompanying regulations to which reference will be made when each aspect is examined in detail.

Part IV: care and supervision

Where the local authority believes that to safeguard their welfare children need to live away from their family, but the family will not agree, or where the local authority does not believe that a voluntary arrangement will safeguard a child's welfare, it will need to apply for a care order (DCSF, 2008). The application is made on the basis that the child concerned is suffering, or is likely to suffer, significant harm if the order is not made (s. 31) (see *Child Protection* in this series: Holt, 2014). When a court makes a care order, or an interim care order, its effect is to give the local authority parental responsibility for the duration of the order, and to allow it to determine the extent to which parents may exercise theirs (s. 33). If the local authority determines that the child's welfare can only be safeguarded by being accommodated away from his or her family, the child becomes looked after under Part III.

Part V: emergency protection

A child can be protected in an emergency by the making of a time-limited emergency protection order by a family (proceedings) court or single family (proceedings) court Justice, with or without notice, under s. 44, or by the police exercising powers under s. 46 (DCSF, 2008). A child placed away from home under an emergency protection order or police protection becomes a looked after child under Part III for the duration of the order.

Statutory guidance

Guidance, issued to local authorities by the Secretary of State for the relevant government department under s. 7 Local Authority Social Services Act 1970, or to each person or body to which the s. 11 Children Act 2004 duty to safeguard and promote the welfare of children applies (s.11(4)), should be complied with unless exceptional circumstances justify different actions. The fact that guidance is issued under s. 7 or s. 11 will be stated in the text. It is commonly referred to as 'statutory guidance' to differentiate its status from practice guidance which is advisory in nature. The statutory guidance relating to powers, duties and responsibilities under the Children Act 1989 is published in several volumes of guidance and regulations. The following are relevant to the exercise of powers and duties in relation to looked after children and will be referred to throughout the text.

Volume 1: court orders

This guidance (DCSF, 2008) provides a complete account of the range of court orders set out in the Act including those that are predominantly used in private law proceedings such as child arrangements orders and **special guardianship** which may provide alternatives to children being looked after by the local authority (see below, Chapter 8).

Volume 2: care planning, placement and case review

Central to work with looked after children, this guidance (DCSF, 2010a) sets out the functions and responsibilities of local authorities and partner agencies under Part III of the 1989 Act and describes how local authorities should carry out their responsibilities in relation to care planning, placement and case review for looked after children. Both the regulations and guidance in this volume are due to be significantly revised in 2014 (DfE, 2013c; 2013d)

Volume 3: planning transition to adulthood for care leavers

This guidance (DfE, 2010b) largely concerns information about the support required for young people who have ceased to be looked after, referred to in the legislation as 'relevant' and 'former relevant' children, so that local authorities can meet the requirements set out in the Care Leavers (England) Regulations 2010. These regulations, applicable in England and Wales, elaborate the increased duties of local authorities to care leavers enacted in amendments to s. 23 Children Act 1989.

Volume 4: fostering services

This guidance (DfE, 2011a) sets out the functions and responsibilities of local authorities and their partner agencies in relation to fostering services under Parts III, VII and VIII Children Act 1989. It also sets out the responsibilities arising from the Children Act 2004 and the Children and Young Persons Act 2008 in relation to fostering services and gives guidance to independent fostering agencies about their responsibilities under the Care Standards Act 2000.

Volume 5: children's homes

This volume (DfE 2011b) provides guidance to local authorities in England and their staff about their functions under Parts III and VI–VIII Children Act 1989. It also gives guidance to providers of children's homes about their responsibilities under the Care Standards Act 2000.

Replacement Children Act 1989 guidance on private fostering

This guidance on **private fostering** (DfES, 2005a) replaces ch. 1 of vol. 8 (Private Fostering and Miscellaneous) of the Children Act 1989 guidance, which was first published in 1991. It incorporates guidance on provisions in the Children Act 2004 and in the Children (Private Arrangements for Fostering) Regulations 2005 and came into effect at the same time as the National Minimum Standards for Private Fostering.

Family and friends care: statutory guidance for local authorities

This guidance (DfE, 2010a) sets out a framework for the provision of support to family and friends carers (currently referred to as 'connected persons'), whatever the legal status of the children they are caring for. In particular, it provides guidance on the implementation of the duties in the Children Act 1989 in respect of children and young people who, because they are unable to live with their parents, are being brought up by members of their extended families, friends or other people who are connected with them.

Provision of accommodation for 16 and 17-year-old young people who may become homeless and/or require accommodation

This guidance (DCSF and DCLG, 2008) must be read in the context of the judgments in *R (M) v Hammersmith and Fulham* [2008] UKHL 14 and *R (G) v Southwark* [2009] UKHL 26 both of which confirmed that the duty under s. 20 of the 1989 Act takes precedence over the duties in Part VII Housing Act 1996 in providing for children in need who require accommodation (see below pages 26–27)

IRO Handbook

This is the statutory guidance for IROs and local authorities on their functions in relation to case management and review for looked after children (DCSF, 2010c). IROs were introduced by amendment to s. 26 Children Act 1989 in 2004 and their position was further enhanced by the introduction of duties on local authorities in regard to the service under ss 25A–C, introduced by the Children and Young Persons Act 2008. The handbook provides guidance to local authorities on their strategic and managerial responsibilities in establishing an effective IRO service and to IROs on the discharge of their responsibilities to looked after children (see below Chapter 7).

Working together to safeguard children

This guidance (HM Government, 2013), which sets out how organizations and individuals should work together to safeguard and promote the welfare of children and how practitioners should conduct the assessment of children, was informed by Professor Eileen Munro's review of child protection (Department for Education, 2011c) and came into effect on 15 April 2013. It replaced *Working Together to Safeguard*

Children (DCSF, 2010a), *The Framework for the Assessment of Children in Need and their Families* (DH et al., 2000), and statutory guidance on *Making Arrangements to Safeguard and Promote the Welfare of Children under Section 11 of the Children Act 2004* (HM Government, 2007).

The guidance is aimed at and should be followed by all from the top to the frontline in all organizations which have contact with children and families: local authority chief executives; directors of children's services; chairs of Local Safeguarding Children Boards; senior managers within organizations who commission and provide services for children and families; social workers; and professionals from health services, adult services, the police, academy trusts, education and the voluntary and community sector.

Key research studies

As in all areas of child care practice, regulation, statutory guidance and national standards, valuable as they are in setting required standards, can only provide the structure of required provision through the imposition of powers and duties. It is the quality of, in this case, multi-agency practice within that framework, informed by research, which makes the difference to individuals.

Leading studies in key areas – placement, foster care, the education of looked after children, reviews and leaving care – will, hopefully, provide pointers to help readers to understand the key role research should play in informing policy development and legislation and, crucially, in improving the practice of managers and workers. Reference is made to relevant studies throughout the text.

Further reading

To get a flavour of the breadth of research evidence readily available, the following texts are recommended for further study.

Davies, C and H Ward (2012) *Safeguarding Children Across Services: Messages from Research.* This overview of 15 major research projects addresses key policy and practice issues across social care and education, health and the family justice system. It helpfully summarizes findings with an emphasis on their relevance to social workers' decision-making in key areas of child care and protection practice.

Jackson, S (ed.) (2013) *Pathways through Education for Young People in Care: Ideas from Research and Practice.* Published more than a decade after the editor's earlier collection (2001) *Nobody Told us that School Matters,* this work brings together, within a coherent structure, a comprehensive range of recent, mostly previously published, research studies which focus, from a variety of perspectives, on the centrality of educational success to the life chances of children who spend all or part of their childhood in care and mechanisms for its achievement.

Schofield, G and J Simmonds (eds) (2009) *The Child Placement Handbook.* This authoritative collection covers a wide research-evidence base across the range of child placement issues. It presents a wealth of knowledge and wisdom in regards, for instance, to: the impact of abuse and neglect prior to placement; the range of permanence options; and the challenges of providing support for the transition to adulthood.

2

ACCOMMODATION UNDER SECTION 20

The routes

A child may become looked after:

- when provided with accommodation through a voluntary arrangement under s. 20 Children Act 1989;
- when placed or authorized to be placed for adoption by a local authority (s. 18(3) Adoption and Children Act 2002);
- when subject to a care order or interim care order (ss 31 and 38 Children Act 1989);
- for a short period of time under an emergency protection order (s. 44 Children Act 1989) or in police protection (s. 46); and
- when subject to police custody, remand, or court orders with residence requirements in criminal proceedings:

This chapter covers issues relating to accommodation under s. 20. The other routes are explored in Chapter 5.

Accommodation of a child in need

Section 20 of the Children Act 1989 sets out the circumstances in which the local authority has a duty to provide a child, but not his or her family, with accommodation. When accommodated the child will become a looked after child, a status which has considerable resource implications for the responsible local authority, not only for as long as the child remains accommodated, but also in supporting the child into adulthood (see Chapter 9)

In order to avoid there ever being circumstances in which a local authority would not have the power to accommodate a child where there is no one else able to do so, the criteria are drafted in all-encompassing terms:

s. 20

(1) Every local authority shall provide accommodation for any child in need within their area who appears to them to require accommodation as a result of—
    (a) there being no person who has parental responsibility for him;
    (b) his being lost or having been abandoned; or
    (c) the person who has been caring for him being prevented (whether or not permanently, and for whatever reason) from providing him with suitable accommodation or care.

Children Act 1989

The decision as to whether the duty to accommodate arises is for the local authority rather than a court to make. The courts generally only become involved where a local authority's decision is challenged as unlawful or unreasonable, though they may do so where the issue in question is whether the individual seeking accommodation is actually a child (see under the section 'Unaccompanied asylum-seeking children' (UASC) page 28 below) or where there is a dispute between local authorities as to responsibility for a child.

> **KEY CASE ANALYSIS**

R (on the Application of A) v London Borough of Croydon; R (on the Application of M) v London Borough of Lambeth [2008]

In this case, Ward LJ set out the questions to be addressed by local authorities when determining whether the duty to accommodate arises; an approach adopted by Lady Hale in *R (on the Application of G) v Southwark LBC* [2009] at [28] (see below at page 26).

The Section 20(1) questions

'(1) Is the Applicant a child?
(2) Is the Applicant a child in need?
(3) Is he within the local authority's area?
(4) Does he appear to the local authority to require accommodation?
(5) Is that need the result of:
    (a) there being no person who has parental responsibility for him;
    (b) his being lost or having been abandoned; or
    (c) the person who has been caring for him being prevented from providing him with suitable accommodation or care?
(6) What are the child's wishes regarding the provision of accommodation for him?
(7) What consideration (having regard to his age and understanding) is duly to be given to those wishes?
(8) Does any person with parental responsibility who is willing to provide accommodation for him object to the local authority's intervention?
(9) If there is objection, does the person in whose favour a residence order is in force agree to the child being looked after by the local authority?' [at 75]

Some of these questions require further examination.

A child?

The duty to accommodate only arises at all if the 'child' is indeed under 18 years of age, an issue which, in the majority of cases, is easily established. With two categories of young people their age is of particular significance: 16- and 17-year-olds and UASCs.

16- and 17-year-olds

If a young person is aged 16 or 17, the duty to accommodate only arises if the local authority considers it likely that the child's welfare will be seriously compromised if accommodation is not provided (s. 20(3)). Many young people refer themselves for accommodation when they fall out with their families.

As we shall see (Chapter 9), if the local authority accommodates a child under s. 20, it then has extensive obligations to the child after the age of 18. These obligations should not be avoided by the local authority

> **KEY CASE ANALYSIS**

R (on the Application of G) v Southwark LBC [2009]

A was a 17-year-old boy asylum seeker from Somalia with indefinite leave to remain in the UK. His mother had excluded him from home. A social work assessment demonstrated clearly that he satisfied all the criteria under s. 20(1), but concluded that he required only help with accommodation provided by the housing authority, rather than being looked after. Judicial review proceedings and the Court of Appeal (Rix LJ dissenting) found in favour of the local authority.

On appeal to the House of Lords, Lady Hale, applying Ward LJ's list of judgments to be made when considering the requirements of s. 20(1) (see page 25 above), concluded that all the criteria under s. 20(1) were satisfied. In those circumstances, the fact that homeless 16- and 17-year-olds may be personally resourceful and also have a priority need under the Housing Act 1996 (Article 3 Homelessness (Priority Need for Accommodation) (England) Order 2002) does not allow a local authority to avoid its responsibilities to a homeless child under s. 20: '[i]t cannot be seriously suggested that a child excluded from home who is "sofa surfing" in this way, more often sleeping in cars, snatching showers and washing his clothes when he can, is not in need' [28].

purporting to accommodate the homeless child under the Housing Act 1996 or s. 17 of the 1989 Act, rather than s. 20 (*R (M) v Hammersmith and Fulham London Borough Council* [2008] and *R (G) v London Borough of Southwark* [2009]).

Following the 'Southwark judgment', the efforts made by local authorities to avoid their responsibilities, addressed in these cases, led to the Departments for Children Schools and Families and Communities and Local Government issuing statutory guidance (DCSF and DCLG, 2008). This guidance makes clear the responsibilities local authorities have towards homeless 16- and 17-year-olds.

Whilst detailing local authorities' responsibilities, considerable emphasis is placed on the benefits of teenagers remaining at home with their families: it is in the best interests of most young people aged 16 or 17 to live in the family home, or, where this is not safe or appropriate, with responsible adults in their wider family and friends network. Local authority responses to 16- and 17-year-olds seeking help because of homelessness should explicitly recognize this and work pro-actively with young people and their families to identify and resolve the issues which have led to the homelessness crisis. This could involve family support such as family mediation or family group conferences. It may be possible for children's services to prevent a young person from having to leave home at all, or it may take much longer to work through significant family tensions and problems while the young person is accommodated by the local authority. It is therefore important that services are designed to enable this family focus to begin on day one and continue throughout the processes of assessment and, where necessary, the provision of accommodation (DCSF and DCLG, 2008:2.1 and 2.2.)

On-the-spot questions

1 Who has responsibility for deciding whether a child should be provided with accommodation under s. 20 Children Act 1989?

2 A 16-year-old says that he can no longer live at home and requests accommodation. What are the local authority's responsibilities under legislation, case law and guidance?

Unaccompanied asylum-seeking children

> The displacement of unaccompanied young people to countries far away from home happens for many reasons, from the need to seek safety from armed conflict, political upheaval or natural disasters, to the desperate escape from deprivation or exploitation by unscrupulous traffickers. What unites them all is the experience of being separated from their families, uprooted from their homes and divided from their culture and all that is familiar.
>
> *Wade et al., 2005: back cover*

A UASC is defined as:

> an individual who is under 18, has applied for asylum in his/her own right, is separated from both parents and is not being cared for by an adult who by law or custom has responsibility to do so. (Home Office UK Border Agency (UKBA), 2013:2)

This definition is subject to the exclusions set out in para. 3 which do not apply if the UKBA has accepted that the child has been the victim of trafficking.

UASCs are owed responsibilities as looked after children. These responsibilities arise wherever the child is living. Local authorities may claim reimbursement of the costs they incur in supporting and caring for UASCs up to a national daily rate published annually by the Home Office, and a grant for the support of those formerly looked after who qualify as 'eligible' for support after the age of 18 (Chapter 9).

There is a lack of consistent national data on the numbers and characteristics of unaccompanied young people being supported by local authorities (Wade et al., 2005: ch. 1). Children claiming refugee status and seeking asylum arrive, some alone, others with relatives or other adults who, once within the UK, are either are not willing or not suitable to care for them. The possible outcomes of an asylum claim are that the young person may be:

- granted refugee status and leave to remain for five years;
- refused asylum but granted humanitarian protection and allowed to remain for five years (most unusual for a UASC);

- refused asylum but granted discretionary leave to remain for three years or until the age of 17.5 years, whichever comes first. Discretionary leave is granted if, at the time of the decision, a return to the country or origin cannot be effected safely;
- refused asylum with no grant of leave. The UASC must return to his or her country of origin.

Whatever the outcome, the UASC will need social work support throughout the claim process (Wright, 2012).

The age of a UASC is peculiarly pertinent and gives rise to particular problems where, in the absence of any identity documentation, establishing chronological age is often problematic.

> **KEY CASE ANALYSIS**

R (on the Application of A) v London Borough of Croydon; R (on the Application of M) v London Borough of Lambeth [2008]

Ward LJ: 'Man or boy? That is the question, easy to ask but not so easy to answer, that is with increasing frequency confronting the social workers of some local authorities because, pursuant to the Age Assessment Joint Working Protocol between the UK Border Agency and the Association of Directors of Social Services, disputes as to age of young asylum seekers are to be resolved by the Social Services Department in order to settle who has to provide accommodation for them. The National Asylum Support Service (NASS) must provide for an adult but the responsibility for a child, ie one who is under 18 years, lies with the local authority by virtue of Pt III of the Children Act 1989.' [1]

Practice in regard to establishing age is technically difficult and can cause deep distress and confusion. The issues are summed up in a recent report which suggests that, ten years after the judgment in *R (B) v London Borough of Merton* [2003] set out the criteria to follow when conducting age assessments, children are still regularly disbelieved about how old they are. This leads to already vulnerable children facing harmful, protracted disputes, during which they frequently do not receive the support and protection to which they are entitled.

> **KEY CASE ANALYSIS** ←

R (Y) v London Borough of Hillingdon [2011]

Y was trafficked to the UK from Nigeria at the age of five to work as a child domestic slave. She had been forced to work for two Nigerian families for nearly ten years, denied access to education, denied medical attention when she was ill, and only allowed to leave the house when the family went to church, when she was forbidden to speak to anyone. Y was finally able to escape her captors in 2008.

After sleeping rough for several weeks, she was taken to the local authority for support. She had no passport, birth certificate or other documentation to prove how old she was. All she knew was that she had seen her date of birth written down in a diary and that it had been confirmed by her trafficker.

For nine months the local authority accepted Y's claimed date of birth. She was placed in foster care and a care plan was drawn up, with no concerns raised about her age by her social worker, foster carer or the teachers at the school in which she was placed.

Following a police investigation during which Y's traffickers told the police that she was older than she claimed, the local authority decided to review her age. Based on a number of factors, including a dental examination and the observation that Y presented as 'independent and astute', the social workers concluded that she was an adult. Y was taken out of secondary school and away from her foster carers and moved into accommodation with adults.

As a result, she was also treated by the Home Office as an adult while the dispute was ongoing. The local authority's decision could only be challenged in court by initiating judicial review proceedings. There was a three-day fact-finding hearing for the court to determine Y's age. The judge believed Y and it is now recognized that she was born in 1993.

The process of being disbelieved and judicial review took nearly three years. As the Coram report identifies: 'yet more time wasted on top of the ten years of her childhood she had already lost. Crucially, while the dispute was ongoing, she was also denied the protection to which she was entitled as a victim of trafficking, such was the focus on her chronological age rather than her needs and vulnerability.' (Coram Children's Legal Centre, 2013:3)

It is widely accepted that there is no single and sure method for assessing a person's age. The – so far fruitless – quest in recent years to find a "magic bullet" that will tell us the exact age of a young person through a single reliable and consistent medical measure has resulted in much focus on the use of X-rays and other invasive and questionable medical procedures. Many NGOs, medical bodies and statutory agencies have raised their concerns regarding the accuracy, legality and ethical justification of such measures.

Coram Children's Legal Centre, 2013:2

Guidance provided by the United Nations Committee on the Rights of the Child (UNCRC) makes it clear that, rather than being for the purposes of immigration control, age assessments 'should be initiated with the genuine and primary aim of ensuring protection to separated children' (UNCRC, 2005: para. 13)

The report quoted above followed the Coram Children's Legal Centre's support for child Y.

On-the-spot question   What are local authorities' responsibilities towards UASCs?

A child in need?

The duty to accommodate only arises if the broad criteria defining 'in need' set out in s. 17(10) are satisfied, that is to say: if he is disabled, or if his health and development are likely to be adversely affected unless the local authority provides services (see *Children in Need of Support* in this series: Westwood, 2014).

The responsible local authority?

For the local authority to have a duty under s. 20, the child in need must be 'ordinarily resident' within the local authority's area. 'Ordinary residence' for children is normally that of her parent(s), with any period living in the following locations being disregarded:

- any place which is a school or other institution;
- under residence requirements in orders made in criminal proceedings; or
- when provided with accommodation by or on behalf of a local authority (s. 105(6) Children Act 1989).

> **KEY CASE ANALYSIS**

Re D (Local Authority Responsibility) [2012]

The issue of 'ordinary residence' was considered by the Court of Appeal in *Re D (Local Authority Responsibility)* [2012]. A teenage mother in the care of Surrey County Council was placed with independent foster carers in Kent where she had lived from the age of 12. Aged 16, while still in care, she gave birth to a daughter and, following concerns, Kent County Council commenced care proceedings and placed the baby with foster carers in Kent. The question arose as to whether Kent or Surrey should be the designated local authority. Application of the principle that the child's habitual residence is that of the mother was complicated in this case by the fact that the mother was placed cross-border. In 'this nice tricky little case' (per Ward LJ at [1]), the Court of Appeal, applying the common law principle, determined, by a majority, that by the time of the application the mother's place of ordinary residence was Kent and that Kent should be the designated authority.

Although this case concerned the local authority designated in care proceedings (s. 31(8) Children Act 1989), the issues in regard to 'ordinary residence' are equally applicable to responsibility for the provision of accommodation under s. 20.

The reason accommodation is required?

The local authority has a duty to provide accommodation if the need arises as the result of:

- there being no one with parental responsibility for the child; or
- her having been lost or abandoned; or
- the person who has been caring for her being prevented, for whatever reason, from providing her with suitable accommodation or care.

The last provision covers an immense range of circumstances in which local authorities may have a duty to accommodate children. They include short and long-term arrangements, circumstances which can be foreseen and planned for, and emergencies. A local authority may also provide accommodation even though a person with parental responsibility for the child is able to provide suitable accommodation. This provision caters for teenagers under the age of 16 who have a 'seriously dysfunctional relationship with their parents' (Bainham and Gilmore,

2013: 489). The essence is that, as with all services provided under Part III of the 1989 Act, the arrangement is made in partnership with families. That is to say with the consent of persons with parental responsibility, unless, of course the child does not have anyone with parental responsibility for them, or they have been abandoned or, being aged over 15, the special provisions for 16- and 17-year-olds apply.

The child's wishes and feelings

> [B]efore making any decision with respect to a child whom the local authority are looking after or proposing to look after, the authority must, so far as is reasonably practicable, ascertain the wishes and feelings of the child ... and give due consideration to those wishes and feelings, having regard to the child's age and understanding.
>
> *HM Government, 2010:1.9*

Here there is a clear divide between children under 16 and those aged 16 and 17 years. The position in regard to the latter, where the purpose of the provisions is to cater for teenagers who may for a variety of reasons have voluntarily made themselves homeless, is clear. Whether or not a parent objects, if the child in need whose welfare the local authority considers 'is likely to be seriously prejudiced if they do not provide him with accommodation' (s. 20(3)) agrees, the local authority *must* accommodate him. It *may* do so, if it considers that to do so would 'safeguard or promote the child's welfare' (s. 20(4)). Also, if a child of 16 or 17 agrees to being accommodated, she may not be removed against her wishes by anyone with parental responsibility.

Children under 16 are in a different position. Although s. 20(6) states that before providing accommodation, a local authority shall:

s. 20(6)

> so far as is reasonably practical and consistent with the child's welfare—
> (a) ascertain the child's wishes regarding the provision of accommodation; and
> (b) give due consideration (having regard to his age and understanding) to such wishes of the child as they have been able to ascertain.
>
> *Children Act 1989*

The duty is limited to 'ascertaining' and 'giving due consideration' not to a right of determination. When this is combined with parental rights in regard to objection and removal (see below), the conclusion has to be that the statutory provisions overrule any considerations in regard to *Gillick* (otherwise referred to as Fraser) competence (*Gillick v West Norfolk and Wisbech Area Health Authority* [1986]. Having said that, paras 1.10–13 of the statutory guidance provide sensitive advice to practitioners in regard to the value of eliciting and responding to children's wishes and feelings (HM Government, 2010).

The right to object to the provision of accommodation under section 20

The essence of the provision of accommodation under this section is that it is a voluntary arrangement. To that end, as far as placing the child in accommodation is concerned:

s. 20

(7) A local authority may not provide accommodation under this section for any child if any person who—
   (a) has parental responsibility for him; and
   (b) is willing and able to—
      (i) provide accommodation for him; or
      (ii) arrange for accommodation to be provided for him, objects.

Children Act 1989

> **KEY CASE ANALYSIS**

Coventry City Council v C, B, CA and CH [2012]

The mother had had a disruptive childhood, suffered significant learning difficulties and was assessed as being devoid of parenting instinct or intuition. The reports on various psychological and residential assessments were uniformly negative regarding her parenting capacity, though not about her as a person. Her first three children had all been placed for adoption. When she became pregnant again, the local authority decided that the baby would be removed from her before her discharge from hospital.

The mother was admitted to hospital as an emergency. She consented to surgery and subsequently to morphine. The social worker spoke to the mother later on that day and she refused consent for the removal of the child. Later still, despite the fact that there was no question of the mother and baby being able to leave the hospital, the social worker encouraged the mother to agree and the child was removed.

The authority sought an order to place the child for adoption and the mother sought her immediate return. The mother and child also claimed against the local authority under s. 7 of the Human Rights Act 1998 for breaches of their rights under Article 8 of the ECHR. The local authority conceded these breaches on the first day of the hearing and resolution in regard to damages was approved.

Hedley J made care and placement orders and dispensed with the mother's consent to adoption. In a commentary on the case, Caroline Bridge reminds her readers that s. 20 appears in Part III of the 1989 Act, involves no compulsory curtailment of parental responsibility, and must certainly not constitute compulsion in disguise. Urging that the judgment should be read in full, she provides a condensed version of the guidance offered by Hedley J, and approved by the President, in relation to obtaining a parent's consent to the removal of a child immediately or soon after birth:

(i)   [e]very parent who has capacity has the right to exercise parental responsibility to consent to her child being accommodated by the local authority under s. 20.

(ii)   The social worker obtaining the consent is under a personal duty to be satisfied that the parent has capacity, and must actively address the issue of capacity and consider the questions raised by s. 3 of the Mental Capacity Act 2005. If there are doubts the social worker should not make a further attempt to gain consent on the particular occasion.

(iii) If the social worker is satisfied that the parent has given consent he or she must also be satisfied that the consent is fully informed. If the social worker is thus satisfied then he or she must also be satisfied that the consent and subsequent removal of the child is both fair and proportionate. Only then, and possibly having taken further advice, including legal advice, should the social worker be satisfied that a fully informed consent had been received from a parent with capacity in circumstances where removal is necessary and proportionate and thus act upon the consent.

Bridge, 2012

Per Hedley J: 'Local authorities may want to approach with great care the obtaining of s. 20 agreements from mothers in the aftermath of birth, especially where there is no immediate danger to the child and probably no order would be made.' [at 46]

Capacity to consent

Section 20(7) refers to the right of a person with parental responsibility to object. However, for the arrangement to be voluntary there must not be any element of coercion.

Further:

s. 20

(8) Any person who has parental responsibility for a child may at any time remove the child from accommodation provided by or on behalf of the local authority under this section.

Children Act 1989

PRACTICE FOCUS

Clare, aged 14, has been rejected by parents who have always been very critical of her and now refuse to let her live at home. She has a 21-year-old boyfriend. Recently she has been aggressive to her younger siblings, frequently truanted from school and stayed out all night. The local authority agreed to accommodate Clare and when in foster care her school attendance improved. After six months her parents are requesting her return, but only if she 'behaves herself'. There is no recognition that their attitude to their daughter might need to be addressed. Clare is confused; she does not wish to lose her family, but would rather not return home.

• What choices does the local authority have?

As we have seen, this does not apply to 16- and 17-year olds, nor do the rights of persons with parental responsibility to object or remove apply where holders of the living element of a child arrangements order, special guardians, or persons with care of the child under an order made in exercise of the High Court's **inherent jurisdiction** agree to the child being accommodated (s. 20(9)). Given the voluntary nature of provision under Part III, where a parent insists on exercising the right to remove against the wishes of the local authority, the authority will have to determine whether its concerns and the evidence to support them are sufficient to apply for an emergency protection order or an interim care order. Without one of these, or police protection, any further detention would be unlawful (see Chapter 4).

Use of agreements with parents

Local authorities frequently rely on written agreements about future behaviour with parents or carers of children on child protection plans. There does not appear to be any research evidence into the effectiveness of these agreements and considerable anecdotal evidence that, while they may help to clarify issues, they do not help to protect the child concerned.

PRACTICE FOCUS

Amy lived with her mother, a single parent until she was seven, when her mother's addiction to drugs and alcohol spiralled out of control and her grandparents agreed to look after her. They subsequently obtained a residence order and Amy has lived with them ever since.

Now aged 13, Amy's behaviour has deteriorated to the point that her grandparents are no longer able to care for her. They ask for her to be accommodated. Amy's mother does not agree with Amy moving to very experienced stranger foster carers.

• Can Amy be accommodated without her mother's consent?

Further reading

Department for Children, Schools and Families and Department for Communities and Local Government (2008) *Provision of Accommodation for 16 and 17 Year Olds Who May Be Homeless and/or Require Accommodation*. For those working with homeless young people or those in dispute with their families, there appears to be a dearth of research evidence on which to draw. This statutory guidance, to which some reference has been made in the text, provides useful detailed information, particularly in regard to the relative responsibilities of housing authorities and children's services.

Wade, J, F Mitchell and G Baylis (2005) *Unaccompanied Asylum Seeking Children: The Response of Social Work Services*. This study provides a rich resource for students and professionals seeking to understand and support UASCs.

3

OTHER ROUTES TO 'LOOKED AFTER' STATUS

AT A GLANCE THIS CHAPTER COVERS:

- care orders
- the choice between accommodation or a care order
- placement for adoption
- emergency protection orders
- police protection
- orders made in criminal proceedings

Child subject to a care order

Since implementation of the Children Act 1989 in 1991, only children made the subject of care orders in care proceedings are properly described as being 'in care'. A care order can only be made by a family court, on the application of a local authority or the National Society for the Prevention of Cruelty to Children (NSPCC) as the only 'authorised person' (s. 31(1)), and may not be made on a child who is 17, or 16 if married. Care orders can only be made on the grounds that the court is satisfied:

s. 31(2)

   (a) that the child concerned is suffering, or is likely to suffer, significant harm; and
   (b) that the harm, or likelihood of harm, is attributable to—
      (i) the care given to the child, or likely to be given to him if the order were not made, not being what it would be reasonable to expect a parent to give to him; or
      (ii) the child's being beyond parental control.

Children Act 1989

'Harm' is defined as:

s. 31(9)

   'harm' means ill-treatment or the impairment of health or development [including, for example, impairment suffered from seeing or hearing the ill-treatment of another];
   'development' means physical, intellectual, emotional, social or behavioural development;
   'health' means physical or mental health; and
   'ill-treatment' includes sexual abuse and forms of ill-treatment which are not physical.

Children Act 1989

Whether the harm suffered is 'significant' is not subject to statutory definition. In some cases, especially those of severe injury, it may be clear, in others less so. Previous statutory guidance emphasizes that:

There are no absolute criteria on which to rely when judging what constitutes significant harm. Consideration of the severity of ill-treatment may include the degree and extent of physical harm, the duration and frequency of abuse and neglect, the extent of premeditation, and

> the presence or degree of threat, coercion, sadism, and bizarre or
> unusual elements.
>
> *DCSF, 2010a:1.28*

If the court finds the 'threshold conditions ' in s. 31(2) satisfied, it will
reach a decision as to whether to make a care or supervision order, a
private law order, or no order, having regard to the welfare principle and
checklist set out in s. 1 of the Children Act 1989 and the 'no order' principle (s. 1(5)). When a care order is made, the local authority acquires
parental responsibility. The parents do not lose theirs, but may only exercise it to the extent allowed by the local authority (s. 33).

Interim care orders

Before the final determination of an application for a care order, a court
may make an interim care order on the basis that there are reasonable
grounds for believing that the threshold criteria set out in s. 31(2) are
met. The effect of an interim order, which may initially be made for a
maximum of eight weeks and then extended for periods of up to four
weeks, is broadly the same as the final order. The local authority acquires
parental responsibility, though the child is not necessarily removed from
home. The court has to decide whether, at a stage where all the evidence
is not before the court, the child's safety requires removal, taking into
account both the risks of removal and the risks of leaving the child in the
parents' care (*Re B (Children) (Care Proceedings: Interim Care Order)*
[2010] at [21]).

On-the-spot question	What are the practical consequences for parents and children of the change in a child's legal status effected by a care order?

Accommodation or a care order?

The Children Act 1989 is predicated on the principle of services
provided for children in need in partnership with their families, and the
avoidance of court proceedings where possible. The question of
whether, in circumstances where there are child protection concerns,
accommodation should be provided under s. 20 or an application be

made to a court for a care order has given and continues to give rise to considerable debate. Soon after the 1989 Act came into force, Masson (1992) raised concerns as to whether the practice of diversion from court resulted in parents feeling coerced into agreeing to the accommodation of their children. The threat being that otherwise they would face care proceedings.

Also, raising concerns regarding the use of accommodation, though on different grounds, the Children Act Advisory Committee, in its final report (Lord Chancellor's Department, 1997), made clear its views on the appropriate and inappropriate use of accommodation under s. 20. It emphasized that accommodation was properly used by local authorities to work in partnership with families, in the spirit of the 1989 Act, in circumstances of need which might include: hospital admission of a parent, bereavement, housing difficulties, and respite care. It was, however, robust in its view that, where the threshold conditions for seeking a care order under s. 31(2) may be satisfied (see page 39 above), because of the very real risk of drift and damaging delay detrimental to the child's welfare, accommodation should not be regarded as an alternative to an application for a care or supervision order. In 2005, Bainham pointed out that the apparently clear distinction between '*voluntary services* and *compulsory care* may be less sharp in

> ### PRACTICE FOCUS
>
> Baby Maria is now aged nine weeks. There was a child protection plan in place pre-birth. Her mother's two older children have been adopted. Maria is currently accommodated under s. 20 in foster care with her mother; the father has contact.
>
> There are a range of concerns regarding the mother and her partner, both of whom have learning difficulties. Mother was diagnosed with a borderline personality disorder at the time of her older children's adoption and a report specified that she would need a lengthy programme of therapeutic support to help her to be able to parent a child. There is no evidence that such a programme has been tried.
>
> The social worker's manager is asking her to consider placing Maria with her mother in a flat.
>
> - Could such an arrangement adequately safeguard Maria?
> - In the circumstances, what alternative arrangements might be considered?

practice than in theory'. He suggested two reasons for this, one princi-
pled and the other practical: firstly, human rights law requires that 'the
least coercive form of intervention which is consistent with the child's
welfare should be the course which is followed'; and, secondly, considerations of the cost of legal proceedings may deter local authorities
from taking children into care (Bainham, 2005: 415). More recently,
Bainham and Gilmore make it clear that this debate is still ongoing
(2013: ch. 12).

Serious concerns have also been raised, and already referred to
(pages 12–13) as to the 'caustic dichotomy between political vision and
the level of human, structural and financial resources' in regard to child
protection proceedings and the provision of accommodation
(MacDonald, 2009).

Children placed or authorized to be placed for adoption

Under the Adoption and Children Act 2002 an adoption agency (all local
authorities are adoption agencies) may only place a child for adoption or,
where it has placed a child, leave her with the persons with whom she is
placed, with the consent of the parent or **guardian** or under a placement
order made by a court (s. 18). Children placed for adoption, or authorized to be placed under a placement order, are looked after by the local
authority (s. 18(3)).

Emergency protection

Two sets of powers, which give children looked after status for the short
duration of the orders, are available to protect children in an emergency:
the first is a court order; and the second involves the exercise of police
powers.

Emergency protection order

An emergency protection order (EPO) may be made by a family court or,
where a court is not sitting, with leave of the justices' clerk, a single
family court justice. The grounds on which an EPO may be made are set
out in s. 44:

(1) Where any person ('the applicant') applies to the court for an order
under this section with respect to a child, the court may make the
order if, but only if, it is satisfied that—

(a) there is reasonable cause to believe that the child is likely to suffer significant harm if—
   (i) he is not removed to accommodation provided on or on behalf of the applicant; or
   (ii) he does not remain in the place in which he is then being accommodated.

Children Act 1989

Subsection (a) provides for two distinct sets of circumstances: the first where the child needs to be removed from a place where he is suffering or likely to suffer significant harm; and the second where removal from a safe place is likely to result in his suffering significant harm. The latter is frequently used to prevent the removal of newborn babies from hospital in circumstances where an assessment has concluded that the baby would be likely to suffer significant harm if removed. These were the circumstances in the case of *Coventry City Council v C, B, CA and CH* [2012] (see page 34 above), although in that case the grounds for making an EPO did not exist at the time the mother was coerced into agreeing to accommodation because she was physically incapable of leaving the hospital.

EPOs may also be made on the grounds that a local authority or the NSPCC are making enquiries on the basis that there is reasonable cause to believe that a child is suffering or is likely to suffer significant harm, and that those enquiries are being 'frustrated by access to the child being unreasonably refused' (s. 44(1)(b) and (c)). On application by the police, a court may issue a warrant authorizing a constable to assist persons exercising powers under an EPO, for instance, by forcing entry to premises (s. 102).

In order to avoid a child having to be removed from her home, if the court has reasonable grounds to believe that by doing so the child will be protected from suffering significant harm, or access to her will no longer be frustrated, an order may be attached to the EPO excluding a named individual from residing in the same dwelling house. The court must also be satisfied that another person living in the child's home is able and willing to care for the child and consents to the exclusion order (s. 44A(2)).

PRACTICE FOCUS

Avril's school is extremely worried about her and has referred its concerns to children's social care. She is aged eight and her school attendance is poor. When she does attend she appears to be dirty, unhappy and steals food from other children. She recently told a teacher that her stepfather hits her and locks her in a cupboard when she is naughty.

When social workers visit her home, the man who answers the door says that Avril is staying with her grandmother. He does not know the grandmother's address and Avril's mother is not at home. When Avril's mother is located, she has a black eye and appears very nervous but says that Avril is safe with her grandmother who has taken her on holiday – she does not know where.

• What actions might be taken to locate Avril?

EPOs may be made for up to eight days in the first instance and, on application to court, may be extended once for a maximum of seven days (s. 45). Unless the child is subsequently made the subject of an interim care order, or accommodated by agreement with the local authority under s. 20, the looked after status will end when the EPO runs out. EPOs are draconian orders that may be made without the parents being given notice and against the making of which there is no right of appeal, though there is a right to apply for discharge of the order if it was made without notice (s. 45). This gives rise to areas of tension between the statutory provisions and the demands of Article 8 ECHR. In *X Council v B (Emergency Protection Orders)* [2004], in an **obiter** judgment, Munby J set out in detail the measures local authorities seeking EPOs must put in place to avoid incompatibility with Convention rights. These measures were strongly endorsed by McFarlane J in *Re X (Emergency Protection Orders)* [2006].

Police protection

If there is reason to believe that a child would otherwise be likely to suffer significant harm, a police constable may take a child into police protection by removing him to suitable accommodation or take steps to ensure that the child does not leave a hospital or other safe place (s. 46 Children Act 1989). Police protection lasts a maximum of 72 hours and, because exercise of the power involves restriction of liberty without a court order, s. 46 sets out very detailed requirements on the police for the duration of the order, one of which is to ensure that the child is moved to local authority accommodation, at which stage he acquires looked after status (s. 21(1) and (2)(a)).

PRACTICE FOCUS

The police are called by neighbours who are concerned that there are very young children in a house where large numbers of drunken teenagers are holding a rowdy party. When the police arrive they find a baby and a toddler on a wet mattress with broken glass all round them. All the teenagers and adults in the house appear drunk and incapable and there is considerable evidence of drug taking. The neighbours say that the children's parents have gone on holiday and left their 17-year-old daughter to look after the children.

- What powers do the police have?

There is concern that police powers, rather than being used as a last resort, may be used routinely in some areas to avoid involving the courts (Masson, 2005).

Children arrested, on remand or subject to orders in criminal proceedings

Children under arrest

Under s. 38(6) Police and Criminal Evidence Act 1984 (PACE), a young person under the age of 17 who is under **arrest**, whom the police wish to detain, must be transferred to local authority accommodation unless it is impracticable to do so. Local authorities have a corresponding duty under s. 21(2)(b) Children Act 1989 to provide accommodation for children under the age of 17 whom they are requested to receive under s. 38(6), regardless of whether or not the child comes from their area (*R (on the Application of M) v Gateshead Council* [2006] at [38]–[45]). The Court of Appeal also held that, in discharging that obligation, the local authority has a discretion, subject to s. 25 Children Act 1989, whether or not to provide secure accommodation (see pages 88–90) in order to prevent the child being detained in police cells.

The circumstances giving rise to the transfer to local authority accommodation being 'impracticable' are narrow, in that neither the young person's behaviour nor the nature of the offence by themselves allow that decision to be made. However, there is an exception to the duty where the request is to place children aged 12 to 16 in secure accommodation and placement in non-secure accommodation would 'not be adequate to protect the public from serious harm' (death or serious personal injury) (PACE Codes of Practice C, n. 16.7), though the lack of secure accommodation in these circumstances is still only a factor to be taken into account. Another valid factor would be physical impossibility because of adverse weather conditions.

Where secure accommodation is available, the local authority must also satisfy itself, independently of the police assessment, as to the risk of serious harm and that the statutory criteria for placement in secure facilities are met (s. 25(1) Children Act 1989, see pages 88–89 below).

Children on remand, or in breach of court orders

Local authorities also have to provide accommodation for children with respect to whom they are the designated authority (s. 21(2) Children Act 1989):

- on remand under s. 91 Legal Aid, Sentencing and Punishment of Offenders Act 2012 (LASPO) to local authority accommodation (aged 10 to 17);
- on remand under s. 91 LASPO to youth detention accommodation (aged 12 to 17) (for details, see Ministry of Justice Circular No 2012/06);
- remanded for breach of youth rehabilitation orders (s. 2 and Schedule 2 Criminal Justice and Immigration Act 2008);
- remanded to secure accommodation for breach of orders made under s. 1(2)A and Schedule 1 Part IV Street Offences Act 1959;
- subject to a youth rehabilitation order imposing a local authority residence requirement or a fostering requirement (s. 1 and Schedule 1 Criminal Justice and Immigration Act 2008).

Annex 5 to vol. 2 of the Children Act 1989 revised guidance and regulations (HM Government, 2010:144–45) provides a handy analysis of changes to a child's care status as a result of criminal justice decisions.

On-the-spot question

In addition to accommodation under s. 20, what are the main routes whereby a child may acquire looked after status?

Further reading

Masson, J (2005) 'Emergency intervention to protect children: using and avoiding legal controls' 17(5) *Child and Family Law Quarterly* 75. This very useful article should help readers to understand the inter-relationship between accommodation on a voluntary basis and compulsory emergency powers. It uses data from two studies to explore the factors that determine the use by local authorities in crises situations of s. 20 accommodation, emergency protection and police protection.

Probert, R (2012) *Cretney and Probert's Family Law* ch. 14, section C provides a clear account of protective court orders with helpful reference to leading cases.

Youth Justice Board: this organization publishes a range of informative literature covering recent developments in the treatment of young offenders. Many are free to download: www.yjbpublications.justice.gov.uk.

4

LOCAL AUTHORITIES' RESPONSIBILITIES TOWARDS LOOKED AFTER CHILDREN

AT A GLANCE THIS CHAPTER COVERS:

- the basic principles set out in s. 22 Children Act 1989
- the concept and responsibilities of the corporate parent
- assessment
- planning principles
- individual care plans
- planning for permanence
- the promotion of educational achievement
- health assessments

The wishes and feelings of and continuing role for the family in the child's life are addressed in Chapter 5, and the range of possible placements is covered in Chapter 6. It cannot be over-emphasized that this division is to a considerable extent an artificial one, designed to help the reader to make sense of the separate elements. In practice, the issues addressed in these three chapters are likely to arise simultaneously, assuming different priorities according to the circumstances of the individual case.

The Green Paper *Care Matters: Transforming the Lives of Children and Young People in Care* (DfES, 2006) spelt out the extent to which the educational achievement, health and emotional well-being of children in the public care, and their subsequent life chances, were, despite earlier efforts, unacceptably worse than those of the general population, and it identified areas where urgent remedial action was required.

Building on responses to the Green Paper and the conclusions of working groups established to identify best practice, in 2007 the government published a White Paper, *Care Matters: Time for Change* (DfES, 2007). This made specific proposals for addressing the multiple life-long disadvantages experienced by children in the public care. The proposals, which required primary legislation to amend Part III Children Act 1989, were enacted in the Children and Young Persons Act 2008 and, subsequently, a variety of related regulations were consolidated into the Care Planning, Placement and Case Review Regulations (England) 2010 (hereafter the 2010 Regulations) which came into force on 1 April 2011. These underpin the statutory guidance: *Care Planning, Placement and Case Review* (HM Government, 2010). Both are due for further revision in 2014 (DfE, 2013c; 2013d).

General duty of local authority in relation to children it looks after

Under s. 22 Children Act 1989:

(3) It shall be the duty of a local authority looking after any child—
   (a) to safeguard and promote his welfare; and
   (b) to make such use of services available for children cared for by their own parents as appears to the authority reasonable in his case.
(4) Before making any decision with respect to a child whom they are looking after, or proposing to look after, a local authority shall, so far as is reasonably practicable, ascertain the wishes and feelings of—

   (a) the child;
   (b) his parents;
   (c) any person who is not a parent of his but who has parental
        responsibility for him; and
   (d) any other person whose wishes and feelings the authority consider
        to be relevant, ...
(5) In making any such decision a local authority shall give due
     consideration—
   (a) having regard to his age and understanding, to such wishes and
        feelings of the child as they have been able to ascertain;
   (b) to such wishes and feelings of any person mentioned in sub-
        section (4)(b) to (d) as they have been able to ascertain; and
   (c) to the child's religious persuasion, racial origin and cultural and
        linguistic background.

Children Act 1989

The corporate parent

The general duty in s. 22(3) places on local authorities the challenging
responsibility to act as a 'corporate parent' for all its looked after children. Some authorities are better than others at ensuring that each and
every councillor understands that this responsibility rests on them as individuals, requiring them to:

   • accept responsibility for children in the council's care
   • make their needs a priority
   • seek for them the same outcomes any good parent would
     want for their own children (DfES, 2003: 3)

As ambitiously expressed in the 2007 White Paper:

A good corporate parent must offer everything that a good parent
would provide and more, addressing both the difficulties which the children experience and the challenges of parenting within a complex
system of different services. This means that children in care should be
cared about, not just cared for, and that all aspects of their development
should be nurtured.

DfES, 2007; LGA and NCB, 2012

Useful training materials for helping councillors to undertake this role are
available (Hart and Williams, 2013).

Care planning

Principles

Social work with children and their families should be underpinned by a cycle of assessment, planning, intervention and review.

> The primary focus of the legislation about children in need, which includes children looked after by the local authority, is how well they are progressing and whether their health or development will be impaired without the provision of services by the authority [s. 17(10)]. The cycle of assessment, planning, intervention and review must therefore focus on the child's developmental progress, including his or her health, and the desired outcomes for the child, taking account of the wide range of influences which affect a child's development both positively and negatively.
>
> *HM Government, 2010:2.15*

The *Framework for the Assessment of Children in Need and Their Families* (Department of Health (DH) et al., 2000) was incorporated into *Working Together to Safeguard Children* (HM Government, 2013). Without the timescales for the assessment process imposed in the 2010 guidance (DCSF, 2010a), it provides the conceptual framework for a multi-agency understanding of the range of factors which impact on a child's life, so that services can be planned to meet the child's needs. A critical part of the assessment process is that of consulting with the child, her parents and other members of the family or involved adults to ascertain their wishes and feelings. In contrast to the earlier guidance, the current *Working Together* emphasizes the need for the assessment to be child-centred. Where there is conflict between the needs of the child and her parent/carers, decisions have to be made in the child's best interests (HM Government, 2013: 36).

The guidance states that the conceptual and practice framework for planning has a threefold purpose:

1 to ensure that children and their families and the child's carers are treated with openness and honesty and understand the decisions made;
2 to provide clarity about the allocation of responsibilities and tasks, in the context of shared parenting between parents, the child's carers

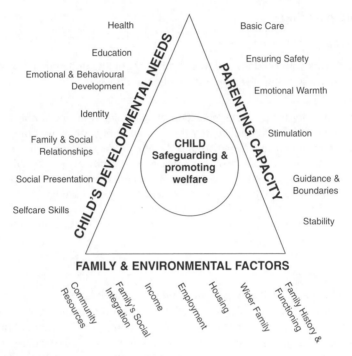

Figure 4.1: Assessment framework

Source: HM Government, 2013:20

and the corporate parents and ensure that actions lead to improved outcomes;

3 to demonstrate accountability in the way in which the functions of local authorities under the 1989 Act are exercised.

The care plan

The arrangements which a local authority must make for looking after a child are set out in Part 2 of the 2010 Regulations. Central to these requirements is the making of a care plan.

> The child's care plan provides the overarching vehicle for bringing together information from the assessment across the seven dimensions of the child's developmental needs [reg. 5] and from any other assessments of the child and his/her family. The health and education dimensions of

> the care plan are populated by the health plan [reg. 7] and the personal education plan (PEP) [reg. 5 (b)(ii)].
>
> *HM Government, 2010:2.7*

Where the child is subject to a care order, a plan under s. 31A will have been approved by the court before the order is made. The s. 31A care plan currently has to be very detailed. When the Children and Families Act 2014 is implemented, it is likely that it will only need to address the permanence plan for the child. The rest of the care planning, covering all the issues below, will be addressed outside the court arena.

If the child is accommodated under s. 20, the authority responsible for the child must, before the child is placed or, if that is not practicable, within ten working days, undertake an assessment and prepare a care plan. The assessment must determine the child's need for 'services to achieve or maintain a reasonable standard of health or development' and the plan must address the delivery of such services. It should, so far as is practicable, be agreed with the child's parents and anyone else with parental responsibility, or, if there is no such person, with the person with whom the child was living immediately before becoming looked after. Where the child is 16 or over and has agreed to be accommodated, the plan should be agreed with her (reg. 4).

Regulation 5 prescribes the content of the care plan, which includes details prescribed in Schedule 1 of the 2010 Regulations.

The care plan needs to be clear and transparent in order that it can be understood by the child (subject to his age and understanding), the parents and wider family, and also the range of professionals and practitioners who may be supporting the child and the family.

The essentials of a care plan

It should:

- describe the identified developmental needs of the child and the services required to meet those needs, including services to be provided to family members;
- describe why a particular placement has been chosen;
- include specific, achievable, child-focused outcomes intended to safeguard and promote the welfare of the child and identify how progress will be measured;

- include realistic strategies and specific actions to bring about the changes necessary to achieve the planned outcome;
- clearly identify and set out the roles and responsibilities of family members, the child's carer and practitioners (including, for example, general practitioner, nurse and designated teacher) and the frequency of contact of those practitioners with the child, his/her carer and/or family member;
- record who has authority to take particular decisions about the child and record any reasons why the making of day-to-day decisions is not delegated to the child's carer (DfE, 2013d);
- describe the contingency arrangements if the proposed permanence plan for the child is not achievable in order to reduce delay. (HM Government, 2010: 2.29)

The plan must also name the child's IRO (reg. 5(d) and see Chapter 7).

The guidance also emphasizes the need for those planning a placement to consult all persons concerned with the child and coordinate the involvement of all the agencies and individuals who are significant in the child's life, having regard to the duty under s. 22(4) Children Act 1989 to ascertain the child's, the family's and others' wishes and feelings. The duty is to 'ascertain' and 'give due consideration' (s. 22(5)). It is ultimately for the local authority to make the decision according to its resources and the child's assessed needs (see e.g. *Re T (Judicial Review: Local Authority Decisions Concerning Child in Need)* [2003]). However, as we shall see in Chapter 5 (page 64), the High Court has emphasized the importance of respecting a child's wishes and feelings (*R (CD) v Isle of Anglesey County Council* [2004]).

The plan for permanence

Permanence is the framework of emotional permanence (attachment), physical permanence (stability) and legal permanence (the carer has parental responsibility for the child) which gives a child a sense of security, continuity, commitment and identity. The objective of planning for permanence is therefore to ensure that children have a secure, stable and loving family to support them through childhood and beyond.

HM Government, 2010:2.3

The guidance identifies the range of options which can deliver permanence for individual children. These include:

- a successful return to the birth family;
- family or friends care, preferably supported by a private law order such as the living element of a child arrangements or special guardianship order (ss 8 or 14A–G Children Act 1989);
- long-term foster care, where it is agreed that the child will remain with the foster carers until adulthood;
- adoption, for children unable to return to their birth or wider family.

Where, in the case of older children and young people, none of the above are possible, the guidance suggests that:

> the care planning process must identify adults such as wider family and friends or other connected people who can provide emotional support and a long-term trusting relationship, which will provide continuing support particularly during periods of transition (HM Government, 2010:2.6).

It is widely recognized that for many looked after children the reality of frequent moves within the care system, or failed attempts at re-unification with their families, militates against the acquisition of any sense of permanence. The performance of local authorities in achieving permanence for children in their care has been widely researched and commented on (for relatively recent examples, see, for instance, Sinclair et al., 2005; Sinclair et al., 2007; Schofield et al., 2007). New regulations and guidance aimed at improving permanence for looked after children are likely to come into force in 2014 (DfE, 2013c).

It also needs to be recognized that some of the ways in which local authorities are required to demonstrate accountability may impact in a negative way on social workers' capacity to undertake the careful assessment of the full range of factors, including research evidence, necessary to optimize decision-making. The timescales for the assessment process may have been removed, but there are still other externally imposed pressures, for instance, in regard to reducing the numbers of looked after children or increasing the numbers of children adopted from care:

> If the pressures to place more children for adoption, and to place them more quickly, undermine the messages from research about the sorts of families who make successful adopters for children in care, the risks will outweigh the benefits for increasing numbers of children. (Thoburn, 2003)

For disabled children, the sad truth is that the chances of permanence are reduced. As Baker (2006) suggests, despite the high level of successful commitment to securing foster placements rather than institutional care since the 1970s, and general acceptance of the principle that there is no reason why family placement for disabled children cannot be successful, disabled children in care may be more likely to be denied the opportunity of the family life that foster care or adoption offers and be more likely to be placed in residential care.

The health plan

The poor physical, emotional and mental health of looked after children when compared with the general population was widely recognized by the 1980s. Scrutiny of the National Child Development Study showed that children in care have many health problems (Lambert, 1983). Fifteen years later, the All Party Parliamentary Health Committee on looked after children found little had changed. It reported that research commissioned by the DH found that 'many looked-after children had undiagnosed chronic health conditions, including poor and uncorrected eyesight, significant weight problems and glue ear. It also found evidence of uncompleted immunisation programmes and courses of treatment.' Mental health was also identified as a particular problem (House of Commons, 1998: paras 252–53).

More recently, statutory guidance applicable to local authorities, primary care trusts and strategic health authorities – *Promoting the Health and Wellbeing of Looked After Children* (DCSF and DH, 2009) – set out best practice in regard to the conduct of assessments and the provision of quality health and dental care for looked after children. It replaced earlier guidance (DH, 2002) which, as identified in the White Paper *Care Matters: Time for Change* (DfES, 2007), was seriously deficient in that it was not on a statutory footing for health care bodies.

Care planning requirements in relation to looked after children's health are now the subject of regulation and guidance (HM Government, 2010: 2.46–64 and Annex 3). Under reg. 7, before the child is placed, or if that is not reasonably practicable, before the first review of the child's case, the authority must arrange for a registered medical practitioner to carry out an assessment of the child's state of health, and provide a written report addressing all the matters specified. A registered medical practitioner or a registered nurse or midwife acting under the supervision of a registered medical practitioner, has to review the child's health and write a report, as above, at least every six months for a child under five years, and at least at 12-monthly intervals thereafter.

Paragraph 1 of Schedule 1 of the 2010 Regulations prescribes the information which has to be included in a looked after child's health plan.

Mental health

> Research shows that more looked after children have mental health problems than other young people, including severe and enduring mental illness. But their mental health needs are frequently unnoticed and unmet. (Richardson, 2002: 1)

As compared to 10 per cent of the general population, nearly 50 per cent of children in foster care and 70 per cent in residential care will be diagnosed with a mental disorder (Meltzer et al. 2003; Green et al., 2005). In addition 70 to 80 per cent of children in care need specialist emotional or behavioural support (Sempik et al., 2008). Providing the right support is often complicated by the lack of a comprehensive service that recognizes that many of these children's attachment and behavioural problems cannot be treated within the Child and Adolescent Mental Health Service (CAMHS) (Rao and Ali, 2010).

The personal education plan

As the then Prime Minister Tony Blair wrote in the introduction to the Social Exclusion Unit's report *A Better Education for Children in Care* (2003: 1):

> Being separated from family and friends, changing neighbourhoods and spending time out of school are difficult experiences for any child. Such an unsettling time makes it much harder to learn. It helps explain why almost half of children leave care with no qualifications at all. It is also a measurement of how society has failed these children in the past.
>
> *Social Exclusion Unit, 2003:1*

As part of the Every Child Matters reforms, the government responded with a variety of initiatives to gather evidence of the poor educational performance of children in the public care (see, for instance, Jackson, 2001). The general statutory responsibility of local authorities was enacted in the Children Act 2004 which inserted a new provision into s. 22 of the 1989 Act:

(3A) The duty of a local authority under subsection (3)(a) to safeguard and promote the welfare of a child looked after by them includes in particular a duty to promote the child's educational achievement.

Children Act 1989

It has long been recognized that disruption to the education of looked after children because of frequent placement and school moves compounds educational disadvantage and poor performance (Pringle, 1965; Harker et al., 2004). Ensuring children in care have access to the best schools through priority in admissions arrangements and a presumption that they will not move schools was spelt out as a key principle in the 2007 White Paper (DfES, 2007) and the latter is enacted in reg. 10 and Schedule 1, para. 2 of the 2010 Regulations. Regulation 10 requires the avoidance of disruption in education, especially in the fourth Key Stage.

As we have seen, the child's care plan must include the arrangements made to meet his needs in relation to education and training – the personal education plan (Hayden, 2005). Schedule 1 prescribes the content, to include:

- details of educational institutions attended, attendance and conduct, academic and other achievements, and any special educational needs;
- existing arrangements for education and training, and other provisions to meet special educational needs and to promote educational achievement;
- any planned changes to existing arrangements, including provision to minimize any disruption caused by changes in arrangements;
- the child's leisure interests;
- the role of the appropriate person, as defined in reg. 2, in promoting the child's educational achievements and leisure interests.

On-the-spot questions

1 What are the essential ingredients of care plans for looked after children?
2 Who might need to understand and help implement the care plan?

Further reading

Berridge, D (2008) *Educating Difficult Adolescents: Effective Education for Children in Care with Behavioural and Emotional Difficulties* analyses the reasons for poor educational performance amongst children in care and explores methods of enabling difficult adolescents to succeed in school.

Golding, K (2010) 'Multi-agency and specialist working to meet the mental health needs of children in care and adopted' 15(4) *Clinical Child Psychology and Psychiatry* 573–87. Illustrated by case studies from one area, Golding provides an overview of the strengths of, challenges in and barriers to the multi-agency working that is essential to meet the mental health needs of particularly vulnerable children.

Schofield, G and J Simmonds (eds) (2009) *The Child Placement Handbook*, ch. 1 and s. III. In ch.1, Malcolm Hill analyses and discusses the benefits and limitations inherent in applying the lessons of empirical studies when making placement decisions. In the chapters in s. III experts in their field analyse research evidence in regard to placement decision-making across a range of specialist areas, including UASCs, minority ethnic and disabled children, and sibling groups.

5

THE VOICE OF THE LOOKED AFTER CHILD AND THE ROLE OF THE FAMILY

AT A GLANCE THIS CHAPTER COVERS:

- the duty to ascertain wishes and feelings
- decision-making authority as between the local authority and parents according to the legal status of the child
- paying due regard to a child's wishes and feelings
- contact between children in care or accommodated and their parents and others
- local authority and independent visitors
- complaints

This chapter examines the legal underpinning of the relationship between the wishes and feelings of the child and the family and the exercise of the local authority's powers and duties in regard to looked after children.

Wishes and feelings

General principles

s. 22

(4) Before making any decision with respect to a child whom they are looking after, or proposing to look after, a local authority shall, so far as is reasonably practicable, ascertain the wishes and feelings of—
    (a) the child;
    (b) his parents;
    (c) any person who is not a parent of his but who has parental responsibility for him; and
    (d) any other persons whose wishes and feelings the authority consider to be relevant regarding the matter to be decided.

Children Act 1989

It should be noted that the duty in s. 22(3)(a) to safeguard and promote the child's welfare does not invoke the paramountcy principle in s. 1(1) Children Act 1989. Local authorities owe duties and responsibilities to large numbers of children in their care and cannot prioritize the welfare of one to the detriment of others.

Legal status of the child

Although the general duty under s. 22 applies to all children looked after by local authorities, the weight given to parents' wishes and feelings, particularly as regards the choice of placement (see Chapter 6), will vary according to the child's legal status. When a child is accommodated under s. 20, the local authority does not acquire parental responsibility, therefore the duty to act in partnership with parents is particularly strong. However, if the child is subject to a care order, although the duty under s. 22(5)(b) applies, the local authority has parental responsibility and ultimate decision-making authority. As the *Tameside* case shows, the right of persons with parental responsibility to determine where a child lives can give rise to real difficulties when a child is accommodated on a voluntary basis because the parents are unable to provide the care required, but they will not agree to the local authority's placement plan.

KEY CASE ANALYSIS

R v Tameside BC ex parte J [2000] 1 FLR 942

J, aged 13, had severe physical and mental disabilities. She had been accommodated by the local authority since she was nine. She lived in a residential home where she received excellent care and was well settled. Her parents were very happy with the placement and strongly disagreed with the authority's plan to place her instead with foster carers. When the authority nonetheless proceeded to introduce J to prospective foster carers, the parents sought judicial review.

Scott-Baker J – granting a declaration in favour of the parents – held that:

1 The definition of parental responsibility in s. 3(1) of the Children Act 1989 includes the right to decide where a child shall live.
2 A local authority that accommodates a child under s. 20 is able to exercise day-to-day powers of management, but a move of the kind envisaged in this case goes much further, into the kind of decision-making that is ultimately exercised by those with parental responsibility.
3 An authority is not entitled to have the last word against the wishes of the parents to place a child who is voluntarily in its care with foster-parents. Where the issue cannot be resolved by agreement, the authority has no power to move the child against the expressed wishes of the parents.

Although this decision strengthens the hands of parents in disputes about a placement for their child accommodated under s. 20, they still cannot dictate to the local authority where the child is to be placed. Ultimately, if the parents refuse their consent to a placement that the authority considers to be in the child's best interests and, as in this case, are unable because of the child's needs to provide care themselves, the authority will have to consider whether it has the grounds to take care proceedings. A care order would give the authority parental responsibility and the right to determine the appropriate placement for the child.

Children's wishes and feelings

> States Parties shall ensure to the child who is capable of forming his or her own views the right to express those views freely in all matters affecting the child, the views of the child being given

due weight in accordance with the age and maturity of the child. (Article 12 United Nations Convention on the Rights of the Child)

In addition to this moral argument as enshrined in international law, Nigel Thomas suggests that there are psychological and practical arguments for listening to children to be a fundamental part of social work practice with children and young people. The former because it is good for young people to have their wishes understood and their views taken into account (see below page 87), and, on a practical level, he suggests that listening to children and young people actually leads to better decisions (Thomas, 2009).

Research into children and young people's involvement in decision-making reveals the extent to which the majority value the opportunity to express their wishes and feelings, and the extent to which really good practice in this area is, as exemplified in the comments from various studies, only experienced by a minority of looked after children (Fletcher, 1993; Thomas, 2009; Timms and Thoburn, 2003; Schofield, 2005; Children's Rights Director for England, 2009; Biswas et al., 2012).

'[W]hat I suggested or said happened and I felt they understood ... They went away and came back a week later and told me what had happened because of what I said.' (Biswas et al., 2012: 3.9)

'They talk about you as if you are not there, so you just shut up and listen without saying a word.' (Fletcher, 1993: 52)

'Social Worker could have explained things better; language used was too complicated for me to understand.' (Biswas et al., 2012: 3.11).

'... using some of my suggestions made me feel happy and gave me more confidence in what was happening'. (Biswas et al., 2012: 3.6)

Children's ability to express their views clearly at reviews, especially if they have any disability, or where they know that their wishes differ from those of the adults in their lives whether parents or social workers, are likely to be increased by their having an **advocate** to speak for them, not only when they wish to make a complaint (see below pages 70–72). Most local authorities commission advocacy services but, for social workers, working with an independent advocate can be challenging:

> The advocate is not there to make life comfortable for the social worker or for the local authority, but to ensure that the child's own views are articulated effectively and to help the child engage in dialogue with the authority and those responsible for providing care. (Thomas, 2009: 76)

The local authority's duty under the 1989 Act is to ascertain wishes and feelings, not necessarily to follow them. There will be many circumstances in which social workers' views of what is in the interests of a child's welfare will differ from the child's view. However, the High Court has made it clear that the decision to override the child's clearly expressed views must be taken on a rational basis taking all factors into account.

> KEY CASE ANALYSIS <

R (CD) v Isle of Anglesey County Council [2004]

C, aged 15, had quadriplegic cerebral palsy. She became a looked after child in about 1994 when the local authority recognized that her mother, a single parent with major health needs of her own, could not cope with meeting C's needs. The authority funded adaptation of C's home and provided support workers to assist in her daily care. They also enabled her to spend periods of time, including overnight stays, in respite care at the home of another family registered as her foster carers. However, their home lacked the physical adaptations needed to meet her hygiene needs.

In 2002, the authority proposed that the arrangements for C's care should change so that she would board four nights per week in term time at her school and spend the remaining time at her mother's house, with substantial input from support workers to aid the mother. C's relationship with her foster family would be limited to contact visits.

C objected to these proposals. She pointed out that no other children spent more than two nights per week as boarders and said that she wished her close relationship with the foster family to continue. Her mother and the foster carers supported her, but the authority then deregistered the foster carers.

C sought judicial review of the authority's care plan.

Wilson J held that the local authority's plan was irrational in that it obviously ran counter to C's clearly expressed wishes and feelings and that a rational plan would take account of the importance of the foster carers in C's life.

Contact

The importance of contact between a looked after child and his family is firmly entrenched in the Children Act 1989 and has been reinforced by the European Court of Human Rights under Article 8 ECHR (see, for instance, *S and G v Italy* (2000)) and is elaborated in statutory guidance:

> The interests of the majority of looked after children are best served by sustaining or creating links with their birth families including wider family members. Consideration of contact is an essential element in the planning process. Managing contact can place emotional and practical strains on all parties involved, which is why there should be clear under-standing from the outset about the arrangements for contact and what is expected of the parents, the responsible authority and the child's carers in connection with those arrangements.
>
> *HM Government, 2010:2.78*

Although the general principles apply to all looked after children, there are important legal differences between the contact arrangements for children accommodated and those looked after under a care order.

General principles in regard to contact

The 1989 Act, Schedule 2, para. 15, regulates the promotion and main-tenance of contact between looked after children and their families:

Schedule 2, para. 15

(1) Where a child is looked after by a local authority, the authority shall, unless it is not reasonably practicable or consistent with the child's welfare, endeavour to promote contact between the child and—
   (a) his parents;
   (b) any person who is not a parent of his but who has parental responsibility for him; and
   (c) any relative, friend or other person connected with him.

Children Act 1989

The authority is also required to keep those specified in (a) and (b) above informed as to where the child is accommodated. In return every such person must ensure that the authority is kept informed of their address (para. 15(2)). Where a child is subject to a care order, her whereabouts need not be disclosed if the authority has reasonable cause to believe that informing the person would prejudice the child's welfare (para. 15(4)).

In order to encourage contact, in cases where visits cannot be made without financial hardship, local authorities may pay expenses to ensure that visits take place (para. 16).

The guidance elaborates the need to consider the child's network and identify those with whom it may be important to maintain or even re-establish contact:

> Care will clearly be needed where there is family or marital conflict, but responsible authorities should be ready to explore the possibility of preserving, establishing or promoting contact which could be beneficial to the child. In doing so they should not overlook problems which may arise when a child is placed with a person who may be reluctant to allow contact with, for example, wider relatives or friends of the child. The child and his/her carers may need support to manage these situations.
>
> *HM Government, 2010:2.81*

Sibling contact

Where looked after children are not able to live with their siblings, the care plan must, so far as is consistent with the child's welfare, set out arrangements for the child to maintain contact with siblings who are also looked after by the responsible authority (Care Planning, Placement and Case Review (England) Regulations 2010 (the 2010 Regulations), Schedule 1, para. 3(1)). Guidance points out that although face-to-face contact may be the most satisfactory way of enabling siblings to maintain their relationship, electronic media can promote positive relationships. However occasional, even in cases where there is no likelihood of a child returning to her family, such contacts may ' keep alive for a child a sense of his/her origins and may keep open the options for family relationships to be re-established when the child is older' (HM Government, 2010:2.86).

Children subject to a care order

Prior to the reforms introduced by the Children Act 1989, local authorities had virtually unfettered discretion in regard to contact (then termed 'access') arrangements between children the subject of care orders and their parents. Care orders, prior to 1991, gave the local authority parental rights and duties to the exclusion of parents, and decisions about parental contact with the child were solely within the discretion of the local authority. Since this was under powers given to the local authority by Parliament, the courts, following well-established legal principle, were powerless to intervene (*A v Liverpool City Council* [1982]). Research demonstrated the extent to which social workers' failure to proactively encourage contact resulted in children remaining longer in care and leaving care isolated from their families and backgrounds (Millham et al., 1986). Apart from their very limited recourse to the juvenile court if access was terminated, parents had to rely on statutory guidance published in 1987. Although the guidance actively encouraged the maintenance and fostering of links between children and their families, research revealed that in practice it was widely ignored (Millham et al., 1989).

Amongst the reforms introduced by the 1989 Act, in regard to children subject to care orders, two were particularly significant. Parents no longer lost their parental responsibility, although they can only exercise it to the extent allowed by the local authority (s. 33 Children Act 1989), and contact with children in care was put on a statutory footing equating, as nearly as possible, the position of parents of a child in care with the non-residential parent under private law.

Section 34 of the 1989 Act sets out a presumption of reasonable contact between the child in care and her parents and others, with recourse to the courts for those specified (s. 34(1)), including the child, dissatisfied with contact arrangements. The strength of this presumption has been regularly endorsed by the Court of Appeal.

The local authority may refuse contact as a matter of urgency for up to seven days if 'satisfied it is necessary to do so to safeguard and promote the child's welfare' (s. 34(6)). There are, of course, cases in which continuing contact is not in the interests of the child's welfare and should be terminated by the court. On an application made by the local authority or the child, a court may make an order to refuse to allow contact between the child and any named person (s. 34(4)). Such an order may be made at the time of the making of the care order or on a subsequent application. Detailed rules regarding s. 34 contact arrangements are set out in reg. 8 of the 2010 Regulations. Where there is a conflict between the local authority's care plan, which involves termination of contact, and the court's view on contact, the court must do what it considers to be in the child's best interests (s.1(1) Children Act 1989; *Re B (Minors) (Termination of Contact: Paramount Consideration)* [1993]).

> **KEY CASE ANALYSIS**

Re E (Children in Care: Contact) [1994]

The local authority wished to terminate contact with a view to placing the children in a closed adoption. The guardian ad litem (**children's guardian**) and expert psychiatrist both supported continuing contact. The Court of Appeal, when allowing the appeal against the judge's order authorizing termination of contact, articulated its perception of the value of contact:

> [Even] when the s. 31 criteria are satisfied, contact may well be of singular importance to the long-term welfare of the child: firstly in giving the child the security of knowing that his parents love him and are interested in his welfare; secondly, by avoiding any damaging sense of loss to the child in seeing himself abandoned by his parents; thirdly, by enabling the child to commit himself to the substitute family with the seal of approval of the natural parents; and, fourthly, by giving the child the necessary sense of family and personal identity. Contact, if maintained, is capable of reinforcing and increasing the chances of success of a permanent placement, whether on a long-term fostering basis or by adoption. (*Per* Simon Brown LJ: 594)

It should be noted that Part I of the Children and Families Act 2014 amends s. 34 and Schedule 2, para. 15 Children Act 1989, to allow secondary legislation to require greater focus on the welfare of the child when contact decisions are made than is currently the case. It will also specify the factors that local authorities must consider when planning for contact between children in care and their families and others. The DfE has published detailed discussion of the policy background to these changes (DfE, 2013a).

On-the-spot questions

Section 34 of the Children Act 1989 radically reformed the law relating to contact between children in care and their parents.

1 What were the reasons for this reform?
2 What is the reasoning behind the proposed amendments to s. 34?

Children placed for adoption

When a child is placed for adoption, or is authorized to be placed under a placement order (s. 21 Adoption and Children Act 2002), previous contact arrangements under ss 8 or 34 of the 1989 Act come to an end and are replaced by contact arrangements made under s. 26 of the 2002 Act. This section will also be amended when the Children and Families Act 2014 comes into force.

Visits to looked after children

The local authority's responsibility

Children placed in foster care and residential placements should have regular visits from their social worker and the opportunity to speak with her alone. Evidence that both the visits and any means of contact at other times were both highly valued by looked after children and, in too many cases, not happening (Morgan, 2006), led to more robust regulation being introduced. Under s. 23ZA Children 1989 Act and Part 5 of the 2010 Regulations, local authorities have a duty to ensure that looked after children must be visited and seen alone. This duty extends to previously looked after children who are no longer looked after because they lost that status when placed in custody (on remand or sentence) in criminal proceedings. Such children have to be visited wherever they are living and be provided with appropriate advice, support and assistance by a representative of the authority.

Part 5 of the 2010 Regulations sets out detailed requirements regarding the frequency, conduct and consequences of representatives' visits. Where the assessment is that the child's welfare is not being adequately safeguarded and promoted by the placement, the responsible authority must review the child's case in accordance with the requirements of Part 6 of the 2010 Regulations (see below).

Independent visitors

Prior to reforms introduced by the Children and Young Persons Act 2008, the appointment of volunteers, independent of the local authority, to visit and befriend looked after children was restricted to cases where either communication between a looked after child and a parent or anyone else with parental responsibility was infrequent, or the child had not been visited or lived with such a person for the preceding 12 months. The appointment of independent visitors is now more robustly regulated.

Under s. 23ZB, the authority should assess whether it should appoint an independent visitor for the child. The basis of the assessment should be determined by the needs of the child, according to factors set out in para. 3.187 of the guidance (HM Government, 2010). The eligibility for appointment is regulated under para. 47 of the 2010 Regulations. The role of the independent visitor is envisaged as being undertaken by volunteers from a lay background although professional child care skills would not rule anyone out. The purpose of independent visitors is to contribute to the child's welfare by promoting a range of developmental needs, encouraging the child to exercise his rights and participate in decision-making, supporting the care plan and the carers, and as far as possible complementing their activities. The function is to advise, assist and befriend, building up a trusting relationship. As the guidance suggests:

> For some children earlier relationships with adults may have ended in disappointment and disillusionment and they may be reluctant to or find it very difficult to establish rapport and trust. The independent visitor must be prepared for the process of establishing trust to be a slow one and for there to be set backs.
>
> *HM Government, 2010:3.190*

Boundaries around the role are set out in paras 3.191–95. Importantly, if the independent visitor has concerns about aspects of the child's case, these should be discussed with the child's social worker or, if still dissatisfied, with the child's IRO (see below, Chapter 7).

Complaints

Since implementation of the Children Act 1989, children and persons with parental responsibility and foster carers on behalf of children have had the right to complain, through a process prescribed in regulations, about the discharge by the local authority of any of its functions in relation to the child under Part III of the Act (s. 26(3)). The process is currently subject to the Children Act 1989 Representations Procedure (England) Regulations 2006.

The process is a three-stage one, with time limits at each stage. It starts with an initial informal investigation, then, if the matter is not resolved, there is a second stage in which the complaint is investigated by an investigating officer, not involved in line management of the case, with scrutiny of the investigation by an independent person. If the complainant is not satisfied with the investigating officer's report, the final stage is for review by a panel of three people independent of the local authority which reports to the director of children's services with findings and recommendations.

In many authorities, the procedure under s. 26(3) is well used by adults, but rarely by children themselves. As Fortin suggests:

Despite looked after children having very clear views about how their lives could be improved they often find it difficult to complain about any aspect of their care (Morgan, 2005). They should be informed about how to use the statutory complaints procedure (ss. 26(3) and 24D) but the assumption that they will feel able to do so underestimates the hurdles they confront. This is understandable in the case of children in foster placements because doing so would make it more difficult to continue living with their carers (Morgan, 2005). Many of those in residential care have emotional and/or behavioural difficulties, and a significant proportion may have been sexually abused. (DH, 1998) Furthermore, countless inquiry reports find that, when re-abused in a residential setting, few children complain, fearing that complaints will go unheeded and that they may be victimized by members of the staff loyal to the abuser.

Fortin, 2009:623–24

Following criticism by Utting, Waterhouse and others of the lack of support for children wishing to pursue complaints (Utting, 1997: 18.10; Waterhouse, 2000: 29.50), the Adoption and Children Act 2002 inserted into the 1989 Act the right to advocacy for children in need and care leavers intending to make a complaint (s. 26A). Advocacy services are normally commissioned by local authorities from independent organizations such as the Children's Society or Barnardo's. A study undertaken in Wales after implementation of s. 26A showed that advocacy support, when received, was greatly appreciated by the children, but needed to be much more accessible and visible to all looked after children (Pithouse and Crowley, 2007).

The only further recourse for a complainant not satisfied with the outcome of this process is to the local government ombudsman (LGO)

> **KEY CASE ANALYSIS**

Local Government Ombudsman Ref (08 016 986) *Children's Services: Child Protection Maladministration Causing Injustice* **21 October 2009**

'Miss Smith' (not her real name for legal reasons) complained that, over a period of several years, she sought support from the council as a child in need but was continually sent away without support being offered. She said the council failed to assess her needs properly and, as a result, did not offer services that she was entitled to. Although the council did eventually assess her as being a child in need and provide some services, she said that this happened too late, those services should have been provided earlier, and she had suffered harm as a result of the delay. In addition to the lack of social care support, she said she was out of school for long periods and the council failed to take action to provide suitable education for her.

The ombudsman found that, although the council's response to the initial contact was appropriate, subsequent assessments of Miss Smith's needs were inadequate. In particular, the council failed to take proper account of her wishes and feelings and took other information at face value.

The council also failed in its duty to work with other agencies involved with Miss Smith. Although the council did in time assess her as being a child in need, this conclusion should have been reached earlier.

As a result of the council's failings, Miss Smith lost out on support that should have been provided to her, thus exacerbating the harm she was suffering as a result of her personal circumstances.

These failings were compounded by the poor handling of Miss Smith's complaint.

Remedy

The ombudsman found maladministration causing injustice and recommended that the council:

- apologize to Miss Smith;
- pay her compensation of £7000;
- review the way it deals with assessments of children in need; and
- review the way it deals with complaints.

The LGO was satisfied with council's response (9 December 2009).

on the grounds of maladministration by the local authority, or an application for judicial review on the grounds of illegality, irrationality or procedural impropriety. The weight of authority suggests that there can be no recourse to judicial review until a complaint has been pursued under s. 26 (*R v Royal Borough of Kingston-upon-Thames, ex parte T* [1994]), although doubts have been raised as to whether, because of its limitations, the complaints procedure provides a suitable remedy (Murphy, 2003). See above for a case where the way a complaint was addressed was clearly unsatisfactory.

Further reading

Coram Voice: committed to getting young voices heard, designed for young people in care or living away from home www.voiceyp.org.

Fortin, J (2009) *Children's Rights and the Developing Law*. Chapter 16 provides a wide-ranging overview of all aspects of children's rights in relation to state care.

Local Government Ombudsman (2013) *C&YP Issues*: this online bulletin (first issue October 2013) publishes details of a range of complaints by children and young people, many featuring local authorities' responses to children looked after or who whom the local authority failed to protect www.lgo.org.uk.

6

THE ACCOMMODATION OF LOOKED AFTER CHILDREN

AT A GLANCE THIS CHAPTER COVERS:

- the range of settings in which looked after children may be placed including
- the statutory context
- connected persons care
- local authority foster care
- residential care
- supported accommodation
- secure accommodation
- children missing from care or accommodation

The statutory context

When a local authority has a duty to accommodate a child, or has decided to do so with the agreement of persons with parental responsibility in order to safeguard or promote the child's welfare, the legal framework of care planning and the decisions that have to be made regarding the choice of placement are set out in ss 22 and 22A–22F Children Act 1989 and the Care Planning, Placement and Case Review (England) Regulations 2010 (the 2010 Regulations). The regulations and statutory guidance on good practice interpretation of the legislation are published in vol. 2 of *The Children Act 1989 Guidance and Regulations* (HM Government, 2010). As indicated earlier, both the regulations and guidance are due for revision in 2014.

Where it is possible that the child will need to be accommodated under s. 20, planning should begin before a child starts to be looked after in order to avoid placements having to be made in an emergency.

> Contingency planning for the possible accommodation of a child while efforts continue to support the family and keep the child at home, may achieve a smoother and more successful and less disturbing transition for the child. (HM Government, 2010:2.26)

This does not apply to children who are the subject of care proceedings where the court currently has to approve the detailed plan for the child before making a care order (s. 31A Children Act 1989). When Part II of the Children and Families Act 2014 comes into force, the requirement for a detailed care plan will be replaced with one specifying whether the long-term plan for the upbringing of the child is:

1 for her to live with any parent or other member or friend of her family;
2 for adoption;
3 or for any other long-term care not within 1 or 2 such as long-term foster care or special guardianship.

Placement

General principles

All placement decisions are subject to the duty on local authorities set out in s. 22(3) to safeguard and promote the child's welfare. In regard to choice of placement, the Children and Young Persons Act 2008 replaced s. 23 Children Act 1989 with new ss 22A–22G. Section 23 had set out the range of options, starting with the family, but without indicating that where possible preference should be given to placement with family or friends, now referred to as 'connected persons', although guidance did so. The 2008 Act amendments made that preference a statutory require-ment. Section 22C of the 1989 Act enacts the principle that wherever possible the child should be brought up within their family. The choice should be:

- a parent;
- a person who is not a parent but has parental responsibility; or
- where the child is the subject of a care order, any person who had the living element of a child arrangements order in their favour immedi-ately before the making of the care order (s. 22C(2) and (3))

unless this would not be in the interests of the child's welfare or reasonably practicable (s. 22C(4)). If that is the case, s. 22C(5), (6) and (7) have the effect of then giving preference to placement with an individual who is a relative, friend or other person connected with the child and who is also a local authority foster parent (s. 22C(6)(a) and (7)(a)). Only if a connected persons placement is not available or in the interests of the child's welfare may placement be made with an unrelated local authority foster parent, or in a children's home regis-tered under the Care Standards Act 2000, or in accordance with any other arrangements which comply with regulations (s. 22C(6)(d) and s. 22D).

In addition to giving preference to placement with connected persons, the local authority must also ensure that, as far as is reasonably practicable, the placement:

- allows the child to live near his home;
- does not disrupt her education (particularly at Key Stage 4);
- enables the child and his siblings who are also looked after by the local authority to live together;
- provides accommodation suitable to the child's needs if she is disabled; and
- is within the local authority's area (s. 22C(7)–(11)).

As statutory guidance recognizes:

Ideally all proposed placements will meet all of these criteria; however this is unlikely to be the reality and social workers, their managers, family placement workers and resource panels may find themselves faced with difficult choices and decisions. The placement criteria are important because most children benefit by being placed with relatives or friends or others connected with them; near their own homes; continuing to attend the same school; living with their siblings and in accommodation which is appropriate for any special needs. However not all these factors are always beneficial for all children; moreover some will have greater priority than others at different times in children's lives.

HM Government 2010:3.10

Statutory guidance provides a helpful elaboration of the issues and competing factors in regard to placement with connected persons, avoidance of disruption in education, placement with siblings, and accommodation suitable for a disabled child (HM Government, 2010: 3.11–27). There is also a wealth of research evidence 'that follows rigorous methodological principles and that can be systematically applied in practice' (Schofield and Simmonds, 2009:1).

Placements out of area

Placements out of the authority's area are subject to the requirements set out in regs 11 and 12 of the 2010 Regulations. The general thrust of these regulations is to provide additional scrutiny of the decision to place a child at what may be a considerable distance from their home. Unless the placement is with a connected person (a relative, friend or other person connected with the child), or a foster carer approved by the responsible authority, it has to be approved by a nominated officer in the responsible authority. The nominated officer has to be satisfied that:

- the placement plan for the child satisfies the requirements in reg. 9 of the 2010 Regulations;
- the placement is the most appropriate available and is consistent with the child's care plan;
- the child's relatives have been consulted, unless this would be inappropriate;
- the area authority and the child's IRO have been notified.

Foster placements	50900
Placed for adoption	3350
Placed with parents	3260
Other placement in the community	4600
Secure units, children's homes, hostels	6000
Total	**68110**

Table 6.1: Looked after children – placements (31 March 2013)
Source: This table only gives an overall picture: a more detailed breakdown can be found in DfE, 2013e: Table A3

The requirements to be satisfied before a placement out of area can be made in an emergency (when a placement is arranged out of hours by the emergency duty team, or must be made on the same day because of current placement breakdown) are set out in reg. 11(3). Further details regarding emergency placements out of area are set out in paras 3.38 and 3.39 of the guidance (HM Government, 2010).

Choice of placement

Connected persons care

The emphasis on care by connected persons, alternatively referred to as 'family and friends' or 'kinship' care, as the placement of first choice reflects policy makers' perceptions of its value in terms of engendering in looked after children a greater sense of belonging, aiding security about their identity, and fostering continuity and stability into adulthood. Research evidence to support enthusiasm for kinship care was initially somewhat patchy, mostly based on relatively small sample studies mainly undertaken in the USA. More recently the evidence base in favour of kinship care has firmed up, although children and young people, giving their views in focus groups convened by the Children's Rights Director for England (2009), were clear that the suitability of family or friends to care for a child should be subject to the same scrutiny as for stranger placements.

Farmer and Moyers' (2008) study, undertaken from 2004–2006, aimed to address the discrepancy between the increased use of kinship care and the lack of knowledge amongst practitioners and policy makers about 'how well these placements work, what helps them to succeed or when they should not be used' (at 13). The results of a range of other research into kinship care, with findings mostly in support, are helpfully brought together by Hunt (2009) whose work informed the summary in Annex B to *Family and Friends Care: Statutory Guidance for Local Authorities (DfE, 2010a)*.

The presumption in favour of placement with family or friends may, as with any presumption, be rebutted. As statutory guidance suggests:

> In some families, the tensions and difficulties that exist or may arise between family members may outweigh the benefits. Some relatives also live hundreds of miles from the child's home. While the chance of developing a secure attachment with a relative may be of key significance to a younger child, the same may not be true of a teenager who may resent being cut off from peer networks or being obliged to change schools at a critical time and lose the local roots which may become a protective factor later on. It is particularly important to discuss the priorities of placement with the child concerned and take account of his/her views. A good relationship between the child, the social worker and the current carer informed by knowledge of the child's past and his/her current needs, wishes and feelings will provide a sound basis for exercising professional judgement within this framework.
>
> *HM Government, 2010:3.13*

The approval of connected persons as foster carers

Except in an emergency, relatives, friends and other connected persons must be approved under the Fostering Services (England) Regulations 2011 (the 2011 Regulations). The *Fostering Services: National Minimum Standards* (NMS) (DfE, 2011d) apply generally. Standard 30, which aims to ensure that family and friends foster carers receive the support they require to meet the needs of children placed with them, relates specifically to family and friends foster carers approved by local authorities or by independent fostering services which approve family and friends foster carers.

Temporary approval of a connected person as a foster carer

In an emergency it may not be possible to fulfil all the requirements of the 2011 Regulations in approving the family/friends carer as a local authority foster carer before, in her interests, placing the child. In these circumstances, regs 24 and 25 of the 2010 Regulations provide for the temporary approval of the relative/friend carer to allow an immediate placement which may last for up to 16 weeks, with the possibility of an extension of up to eight weeks (para. 25). Before giving temporary approval, a basic assessment of the suitability of the connected person, other adults resident with him/her, and the accommodation must be undertaken (para. 24(2) and Schedule 4).

Statutory guidance on family and friends care (DfE, 2010a) is aimed at ensuring that children and young people who are looked after by family members or friends because they are unable to live with their parents receive the support that they and their carers need to safeguard and promote their welfare. The guidance is not restricted to looked after children. It additionally addresses the service needs of children and young people and their kinship carers living in a variety of arrangements where the child is not looked after:

- informal arrangements with a relative;
- informal arrangements with friends or other family members which last for a period of fewer than 28 days;
- private fostering arrangements (as above but lasting for more than 27 days) (see Chapter 8);
- children subject to the living elements of a child arrangements order or special guardianship order (see Chapter 8); or
- arrangements which may lead to an adoption order.

Financial arrangements for connected persons care

Statutory guidance (DfE, 2011a:5.71) requires foster parents to be given 'clear information about the criteria for making financial payments to them, including allowances, fees and other expenses'. This is also spelt out in the NMS (DfE, 2011d) which set a baseline and are used by the Office for Standards in Education, Children's Services and Skills (Ofsted) when undertaking inspections:

> Each foster carer receives at least the national minimum
> allowance for the child, plus any necessary agreed expenses for
> the care, education and reasonable leisure interests of the child,
> including insurance, holidays, birthdays, school trips, religious
> festivals etc, which cover the full cost of caring for each child
> placed with her/him. (NMS, DfE, 2011d:28.1)

There is a long history of local authorities paying kinship carers at a lower
rate than stranger foster carers (see, for instance, the robust comments
of Munby, J in *R (L) v Manchester City Council* [2001]). The guidance is
now very clear:

> Criteria for calculating fees and allowances must apply equally to
> all foster carers, whether the foster carer is related to the child or
> unrelated, or the placement is short or long term. (DfE, 2011a:5.71;
> NMS, DfE, 2011d:28)

Despite this clear articulation of principle, local authorities may, as is illustrated by the following key case (page 82), try to argue that in regard to
family carers there may be 'cogent reasons' for departing from statutory
guidance and the NMS.

Arrangements for a child subject to a care order to be
placed with parents

When a court makes a care order, the local authority acquires parental
responsibility for the child, which includes the power to determine where
the child will live. The parents do not lose their parental responsibility, but
can only exercise it to the extent allowed by the local authority (s. 33
Children Act 1989). The placement of a child subject to a care order with
his parent(s) is subject to special regulation (2010 Regulations, Part 4, regs
15–20), although a child on an interim care order may be allowed to
remain with the parent pending a final hearing. Any decision to place a
child subject to a care order back with a parent under the 2010 Regulations
must not be incompatible with a court order relating to contact made
under s. 34 Children Act 1989. It will also be subject to the requirement for
a placement plan and review in accordance with the 2010 Regulations.

Guidance indicates that where a local authority decides that placement
of a child subject to a care order with parents is an appropriate way to
discharge its duty under s. 22C Children Act 1989, it should also consider

> **KEY CASE ANALYSIS**

R (X) v London Borough of Tower Hamlets [2013]

Three severely damaged siblings were placed with their aunt after no other foster carer could be found. After a detailed assessment, she was approved as a foster carer and reviews demonstrated her commitment and provision of excellent care.

It was the authority's policy, on the basis that the roles were different, to pay less in fees and allowances, save in 'exceptional circumstances', to family foster carers than to unrelated foster carers. The aunt claimed that the differential treatment of family as compared to unrelated foster carers was unlawful, as a matter of domestic law and because it constituted unlawful discrimination contrary to Article 14 ECHR.

Declaring the authority's fostering policies unlawful, the judge held:

1 The local authority's fostering policies were unlawful to the extent that they discriminated on the grounds of pre-existing relationship with the child between family and unrelated foster carers in the payment of the fostering fee and the reward element of payments made to carers of children with disabilities.
2 Local authorities' freedom to determine their own policies is constrained by their having to have a cogent reason not to follow the statutory guidance.
3 It was clearly contrary to the guidance that the claimant received less as a family foster carer than as an unrelated foster carer for the same children. The authority's policies on fees were not in accordance with the statutory guidance to the extent that they provided for different treatment of family and unrelated foster carers.

The judge did not consider it necessary to pursue the ECHR issue.

The decision was upheld by the Court of Appeal: *London Borough of Tower Hamlets v The Queen on the Application of X* [2013].

whether the care order is still required. If the authority and the parent agree that an application to discharge the care order is appropriate:

> [S]uch an agreement must include both the level of support and supervision by the responsible authority and co-operation by the parent, with the commitment of all involved to working together in the child's best interests. (HM Government, 2010:3.67)

Careful attention also has to be paid to the parents' suitability to care for the child on the basis that the care order could not have been made unless a court found the threshold conditions for making the order satisfied (s. 31(2) Children Act 1989). In practice, such arrangements very often involve a written agreement between the local authority and the parent. Unfortunately, despite the prevalence of the use of written agreements both in these circumstances and others where social workers are working with families without court orders, their efficacy appears deeply under-researched.

Research into the outcomes for neglected children returned to their families suggests that achieving lasting change in abusive and neglectful families is particularly problematic and may result in very poor outcomes for the children (Farmer and Lutman, 2010; Davies and Ward, 2012, ch. 4). Before a decision is made to place a child back with parents, the local authority nominated officer has to be satisfied that the child's wishes and feelings have been ascertained, the parent(s) has/have been assessed as suitable, the IRO has been consulted, the placement will safeguard and promote the child's welfare (DfE, 2011a:3.76), and that return will be in the child's best interests (DfE, 2011a:3.77 and 3.78).

PRACTICE FOCUS

Two boys aged five and four and a girl aged two, all with complex needs whose mother suffered mental health problems, were made the subject of care orders on the basis of neglect and the domestic violence perpetrated by their father who belonged to a family heavily involved in criminal activity and was described as 'very scary'. The boys were placed together and the girl separately in foster care. The girl was subsequently adopted. The boys, who had spasmodic contact with their parents and sister, did well in their foster home. When they were aged nine and ten their parents indicated that they wished the boys to be returned to their care.

- What factors, including evidence from research, will social workers need to bear in mind when considering the rehabilitation of these boys with their parents?
- If it is decided to return the boys and apply for discharge of the care order, what other legal safeguard might be considered?

Other accommodation for looked after children

The range of possible placements

> Securing sufficient accommodation that meets the needs of looked after children is a vital step in delivering improved outcomes for this vulnerable group. Having the right placement in the right place, at the right time, is a vital factor in improving placement stability, which in turn is a critical success factor in relation to better outcomes for looked after children.
>
> *DCSF, 2010b:1.7*

The concept of improving services for looked after children by placing the so-called 'sufficiency duty' on local authorities was proposed in the White Paper *Care Matters: Time for Change* (DfES, 2007) and enacted in the Children and Young Persons Act 2008 which introduced s. 22G into the Children Act 1989. Section 22G places a duty on local authorities to secure, so far as reasonably practicable, sufficient accommodation within the authority's area which meets the needs of children that the local authority is looking after, and whose circumstances are such that it would be consistent with their welfare for them to be provided with accommodation that is in the local authority's area.

Statutory guidance amplifies the duty, indicating that existing good practice (illustrated by case studies) suggests that the provisions set out in the 1989 Act can best be met through the development of new commissioning practices in which local authorities work with their Children's Trust partners to:

- support and maintain diversity of services to better meet the needs of looked after children including through the provision of preventive and early intervention services to reduce the need for care proceedings;
- place children within their local authority area where reasonably practicable and where this is consistent with a child's needs and welfare;
- support the market to deliver more appropriate placements and other services locally;
- have mechanisms for commissioning appropriate, high quality placements and services outside of their local area, which can meet a child's identified needs (this will be necessary in circumstances where

> it is not consistent with a child's welfare or reasonably practicable for him/her to be placed within the local area); and
> - have in place a strategy for addressing supply issues and reducing constraints.
>
> *DCSF, 2010b:2.7*

A standard for good commissioning practice is set out in ch. 4 of the guidance. The range of placements has to cover a wide spectrum: those suitable for short breaks and emergencies, long-term foster care and adoption, residential care and secure accommodation, and, when the Children and Families Act 2014 reforms are implemented, fostering for adoption. Commissioning arrangements have to cover a number of factors relating to the assessed needs of individual children. Consideration of the main placement choices follows.

Placement with local authority foster parents

When a local authority determines that placement with family or friends is not available or not in the interests of a looked after child's welfare the choice will be made on the basis of the child's assessed needs. It does, however, have to be recognized that practical limitations on choice are likely to play a part in any decision. Compliance with the 'sufficiency duty' can never ensure that the ideal placement is available.

The possibility of the child needing accommodation is probably most helpfully regarded as part of a continuum of family support services, rather than to be seen as a last resort. Such an approach, with careful assessment and advance planning before placement, gives, guidance suggests, the greater chances of securing a more successful and less disturbing transition to a foster placement if the child has to be accommodated (HM Government, 2010:3.81).

The 2011 Regulations as amplified by statutory guidance (DfE, 2011a) require the local authority to comply with a range of conditions before a placement with a local authority foster carer can be made:

- the foster carer must be approved by the local authority fostering panel or by another fostering services provider, provided the provider and any other local authority which currently has another child placed with the foster carer consent. In addition the detailed requirements regarding the approval of foster carers set out in reg. 27 of the 2011 Regulations must be complied with;

- the terms of the foster care approval are consistent with the proposed placement; and
- the foster carer has entered into a foster care agreement in accordance with reg. 27(5).

In an emergency, a child may be placed with any approved local authority foster carer for a maximum of six days even if the terms of the approval are not consistent with the placement. After six days the child must be removed unless the terms of approval have been amended to be consistent with the placement (2010 Regulations, reg. 23(1) and (2)).

Whilst the regulations set out the legal framework and the NMS the minimum standards acceptable for a foster care service, the statutory guidance provides a detailed framework for practice. There is also a wealth of research-based literature to inform decision-making in this area (see, for instance, Schofield and Beek, 2005; Sinclair, 2005; Schofield et al., 2007).

Fostering for adoption

Building on the perceived success of concurrent planning for babies and very young children whereby, whilst the possibility of their rehabilitation with the birth family is assessed, the child is fostered by approved prospective adopters (Laws et al., 2012), the Children and Families Act 2014 amends s. 22C Children Act 1989. Local authorities considering adoption for a looked after child will be required to place the child with a local authority foster parent who has also been approved as a prospective adopter.

Residential care

Guidance suggests that placement in residential care, although in the main more suitable for older children, should be considered as a potential placement option alongside other options (HM Government, 2010:3.96).

> It is essential that residential care is seen as part of the overall network of services for children and is used in a planned way when it is in the child's best interests. Residential care is, and will remain, a vital resource for looked after children. (DfE, 2011b: 1.24)

The term 'residential care' covers a wide range of different provisions, including: children's homes of various sizes and regimes, secure children's homes, residential schools, care homes, assessment centres and youth treatment centres. The current level of knowledge about the state of residential child care and the characteristics of children and young people in residential care has been the subject of research studies (Clough et al., 2006; Sinclair et al., 2007).

Those managing residential establishments have to be registered under the Care Standards Act 2000, unless one of the exemptions, relating to specific institutions or those providing short-term accommodation for educational or recreational purposes, set out in reg. 3 of the Children's Homes Regulations (England) 2001, apply.

Children's homes are subject to the Care Standards Act 2000, the Children's Homes (England) Regulations 2001 as amended in 2011, and vol. 5 of the *Children Act 1989 Guidance and Regulations* that underpin the NMS which are the benchmark for Ofsted inspections. The NMS are aimed at providers and Ofsted focuses on securing positive welfare, health and education outcomes for looked after children (DfE, 2011b).

A significant proportion of looked after children placed in children's homes are teenagers who have different placement needs to younger children and may express a preference for living in residential care, or may need the specialist care provided in a therapeutic environment, either on a long-term basis or as part of a planned transition into a more familial setting. A large sample study of the English care system found that residential schools hardly ever cater for children under the age of 11, residential units only do so very rarely, and that, in general, placements in residential units were of significantly shorter duration than kinship or foster placements (Sinclair et al., 2007).

Boys outnumber girls by 63 per cent to 37 per cent in residential care and over a quarter of all those placed have had at least five previous placements (DfE, 2013b). Sinclair and his colleagues also found that children in residential care differ from those looked after in other ways: they are more likely to be disabled, have suffered acute family stress and manifest difficult behaviour; they all had worse school performance and higher challenging behaviour scores (Sinclair et al., 2007).

It should be noted that, applying the decision in relation to housing in *R (on the Application of G) v Southwark LBC* [2009], where a child in need is placed in a residential special school which will meet both his social care and educational needs, the local authority cannot avoid its continuing responsibilities to him when he reaches the age of 18 (see Chapter 9) by claiming that the placement is made under the Education

Act 1996, rather than the Children Act 1989 (*R (O) v East Riding of Yorkshire (Secretary of State for Education Intervening)* [2011].

Characteristics of children's homes

The numbers of children placed in children's homes – 7 per cent of placements nationally – varies very widely between local authorities with more than half of these placements being outside the local authority area. The private and voluntary sector now provides 78 per cent of the children's homes on the Ofsted register. Local authority homes tend to be slightly larger with an average of 5.8 places as compared with an average of 4 in private/voluntary homes. Evidence does not suggest any clear distinction as to the quality of provision, as assessed by Ofsted, as between public or private or in relation to the size of the home (DfE, 2013b).

Supported accommodation

Residential accommodation in which looked after children receive some support may or may not be subject to registration depending on whether the staff are primarily responsible for residents' care, or residents are generally able to assume responsibility for themselves. Annex B of the Children's Homes Guidance (DfE, 2011b) helpfully sets out a sequence of questions which aid decision-making as to whether care is provided at a level to require registration.

Secure accommodation

Restricting the liberty of looked after children is subject to statutory regulation under s. 25 Children Act 1989, and human rights law requirements (Parry, 2000; Fortin, 2001; Stather, 2013). The welfare use of accommodation provided for the purposes of restricting the liberty of looked after children, as compared with use in criminal proceedings, is subject to statutory provision in terms of the circumstances in which children may be placed in a secure children's home and the maximum periods for which restriction may last. The criteria for restricting a child's liberty on welfare grounds are set out in s. 25(1) Children Act 1989:

s. 25(1)

    (a) that—
        (i) he has a history of absconding and is likely to abscond from any other description of accommodation; and

(ii) if he absconds he is likely to suffer significant harm; or

(iii) that if he is kept in any other description of accommodation he is likely to injure himself or any other persons.

Children Act 1989

The use of secure accommodation is also subject to the Secure Accommodation Regulations 1991.

If the criteria are satisfied, a child over the age of 12 may be kept in secure accommodation for up to 72 hours without a court order. Children under the age of 13 may only be placed in secure accommodation with the direct authority of the Secretary of State.

Secure accommodation orders

In order to restrict a child's liberty for more than 72 hours, or an aggregate of 72 hours in a 28-day period, the local authority must obtain a court order on the basis that the criteria in s. 25 Children Act 1989 are satisfied. Applications are made in the family court. If a court finds the s. 25(1) criteria are met, the making of the order is mandatory (s. 25(4)). As the proceedings come under Part III of the 1989 Act, the child's welfare is not the court's paramount consideration (*Re M (A Minor) (Secure Accommodation Order)* [1995]).

The order may be made for up to three months in the first instance and subsequently for periods of up to six months, but only up to the maximum considered necessary (*Re W (A Minor) (Secure Accommodation Order)* [1993]) and only if the local authority continues to believe the criteria to be met *(Re LM v Essex County Council* [1999]). Orders are often made for shorter periods. Over a generation, there has been increasing recognition that, because the restriction of liberty is involved, children ought to be allowed to attend secure accommodation order hearings if they wish to do so. In a recent case it was decided that a very angry and disturbed 13-year-old girl should be allowed to attend a hearing to extend her order for three months, despite the local authority, the children's guardian and the unit in which she was accommodated opposing her attendance *(A City Council v T, J and K (by her Children's Guardian* [2011]).

Whereas earlier guidance suggested that secure accommodation should only be used as a last resort, and a small sample survey of local authorities commissioned in 2005 suggested that most followed the guidance and tried alternative therapeutic placements instead (Jane Held Consulting Ltd, 2006), current statutory guidance adopts a different approach:

Restricting the liberty of children is a serious step which should only be taken where the needs of the child cannot be met by a more suitable placement elsewhere. However, it should not be considered as a 'last resort' in the sense that all other options must have been tried without success. Such an approach could lead to the inappropriate placement of children and young people in the community, where their needs may not be met, possibly with highly adverse consequences, both for such children and young people themselves and the wider community.

DCSF, 2008:5.2

PRACTICE FOCUS

Fleur, aged 13, was accommodated at age ten when her mother was no longer able to care for her due to her own mental health and substance abuse problems. Three foster placements broke down when Fleur's carers could not manage her disruptive behaviour and she was placed in a children's home which does not have a secure facility. Recently she has failed to attend school and has absconded from the home on a regular basis, stayed away overnight and returned with expensive electronic gadgets. Children's services have received reports of Fleur being seen in the company of several older men. She insists that one of them is her boyfriend and looks after her. Fleur's social worker and the home staff believe that she is at high risk of sexual exploitation but feel powerless to control her.

• Would this case meet the criteria for a secure accommodation order?

Secure children's homes contain children placed under orders in criminal proceedings as well as on welfare grounds under the Children Act 1989. When s. 25 came into force in 1991, the numbers of children in secure accommodation dropped and many very expensive secure resources were closed. As a result there are now only 16 secure establishments in England and Wales, putting pressure on places, and resulting in a number of extremely vulnerable children having to be placed a very long way from friends and family; a possible breach of their rights under Article 8 ECHR (Pickford and Dugmore, 2012: ch. 1).

Children missing from care or accommodation

> Going missing is a key indicator that a child might be in great danger. When children go missing, they are at very serious risk of physical abuse, sexual exploitation and sometimes so desperate they will rob or steal to survive. (All Party Parliamentary Group, 2012)

When a child who is subject to a care order is abducted or enticed away from care, there are are statutory provisions to enable recovery of the child and punishment of those responsible (ss 49–51 Children Act 1989). Apart from the few who fall within these provisions, this important safeguarding issue is dependent on effective local multi-agency working, especially between the police and local authorities, monitored by LSCBs.

There is little reliable data on the numbers of children who go missing, although Ofsted estimates that looked after children are three times more likely to go missing than children living at home (2013). Inspectors also found that local authority responses were varied. They found evidence in some authorities of high quality multi-agency working addressing prevention, swift responses and sensitive follow-up, but also some poor practice and a general lack of a strategic approach to address the needs of missing children.

New statutory guidance draws together these developments with a useful list of online resources in Annex B (DfE, 2013f).

Further reading

Fortin, J (2009) *Children's Rights and the Developing Law*. Chapter 16 'Right to protection in state care and to state accountability' provides analysis and discussion of the legal and practice tensions between statutory child protection and human rights issues.

Schofield, G and J Simmonds (eds) (2009) *The Child Placement Handbook*. This collection brings together research and authoritative comment across a diverse range of child placement issues, including: the impact of histories of abuse and neglect on children in placement; reunification with birth families; permanence in foster care; and the placement of unaccompanied asylum-seeking children.

Stather, J (2013) *Secure Accommodation Handbook*. This book, mainly aimed at lawyers, and focusing on applications to court, is included because it provides a comprehensive account of current provisions and the human rights requirements of decision-making in regard to the use of secure accommodation. There are useful case summaries and a comprehensive appendix of all the relevant statutory material.

7

REVIEWS

AT A GLANCE THIS CHAPTER COVERS:

- steps in the development of reviews and the IRO service
- the regulation of reviews and the responsibilities of IROs under regulations and guidance
- the sparse research findings on the efficacy of the system
- commentary on the few reported cases
- possible developments following recommendations in the Family Justice Review

Reviews are a key component in the virtuous cycle of assessment, planning, intervention and review which should enable corporate parents to improve the outcomes for looked after children.

> The purpose of reviews is to monitor the progress of achieving the outcomes set in the care plan and to make decisions to amend the plan as necessary in light of changed information and circumstances. Reviews take place in order to ensure that the child's welfare continues to be safeguarded and promoted in the most effective way throughout the period that s/he is looked after.
>
> *HM Government, 2010:4.1*

Origins of the IRO service

The review of Children's Cases Regulations 1991, which were replaced in April 2011 by the Care Planning, Placement and Case Review (England) Regulations 2010 (the 2010 Regulations) placed a duty on local authorities to regularly review the case of each looked after child, taking the views of the child, parents and others into consideration. The child and the others detailed had to be notified of decisions taken at review which had to be recorded and implemented. Initially, reviews were undertaken by social workers without any requirement for an independent scrutiny of the process or outcome of reviews. Over the years, the courts have expressed considerable frustration in regard to their lack of any power, once a care order was in place, to intervene to require local authorities to follow the care plan on the basis of which a care order had been made (see, for instance, *Re T (A Minor)(Care Order: Conditions)* [1994]; *Re S and D (Children: Powers of Court)* [1995]). Once the Human Rights Act 1998 was in force, the Court of Appeal identified that looked after children whose parents or guardians were unable or unwilling to question care decisions made by the local authority had no effective remedy if the local authority failed to meet its statutory duty towards them.

Creative judicial remedies were pursued: in the Court of Appeal these included the introduction of 'starred milestones' (*Re W and B; Re W (Care Plan)* [2001]). Although agreeing with Lord Nicholls in rejecting the Court of Appeal's efforts as being clearly contrary to the intention of Parliament as expressed in the Children Act 1989, their Lordships were sympathetic to its objectives. Lord Mackay of Clashfern, recognizing the need for external review of local authorities' functions in respect of children in care, said:

> I would strongly urge the government and Parliament to give urgent attention to the problems … so that we do not continue failing some of our most vulnerable children. (*Re S (Minors) (Care Order: Implementation of Care Plan; Re W (Minors) (Care Order: Adequacy of Care Plan)* [2002] at 112)

The government responded, through an amendment to s. 26 of the Children Act 1989 in the Adoption and Children Act 2002, by requiring local authorities to appoint IROs to review the care plans for all looked after children. That Act also introduced a new procedure under s. 31A of the 1989 Act for the judicial scrutiny of care plans in care proceedings. Provision was also made, in cases where the s. 31A care plan was not being followed and negotiation had failed, for, as a last resort, referral to the **Children and Family Courts Advisory and Support Service (CAFCASS)** for dispute resolution or legal action. CAFCASS's functions were extended so that on referral from an IRO it could bring legal proceedings including judicial review and claims for breaches of the child's human rights. It should be noted that, because this reform applied to all looked after children, it went much further than addressing the needs of children with no one to speak for them.

The criteria for the appointment and responsibilities of IROs were set out in the Review of Children's Cases (Amendment) (England) Regulations 2004 and the IROs' guidance (DCSF, 2010c). However, considerable concerns regarding the effectiveness of the IRO initiative were expressed in the Green Paper *Care Matters* (DfES, 2006). In particular it identified that:

- IROs were not sufficiently robust in challenging decisions made by local authorities even where professional practice was obviously poor;
- not every statutory review was being conducted in a way that encouraged a challenging analysis of the proposals for meeting the child's needs;
- insufficient weight was being given to the views of the child or to those of his parents, carers, or other professionals with a role in securing his welfare;

- unless care plans are rigorously examined, the review is no longer an opportunity for informed reflection on the child's progress and planning for the child's future; instead it becomes merely a sterile 'box ticking' exercise.

Very few cases were referred to CAFCASS (11 to November 2011) and none resulted in legal proceedings giving rise to a reported case (Knowles and Sharpe, 2012) . However, in *S (A Child Acting by the Official Solicitor) v Rochdale Metropolitan Borough Council and the Independent Reviewing Officer* [2008] robust criticism was expressed on behalf of the Official Solicitor referring to the IRO in the case as having been 'impotent or supine' (at 95) in neglecting to challenge the local authority's failure to ensure that anyone was exercising parental responsibility for an extremely vulnerable 16-year-old.

Following consultation, the White Paper *Care Matters: Time for Change* (DfES, 2007) proposed the reforms which were enacted in s. 10 Children and Young Persons Act 2008 in force since April 2011.

Current requirements

The present responsibilities of local authorities regarding reviews of looked after children's cases and the role of IROs are governed by Part 6 of the 2010 Regulations and the *IRO Handbook* (DCSF, 2010c).

In general

Local authorities have a duty:

- to review the child's case, as prescribed;
- not, unless it is not reasonably practicable, to make any significant change in the child's care plan unless the proposed change has first been considered at a review.

Reviews under Part 6 may be undertaken at the same time as other reviews, assessment or consideration of the child's case, for instance, by the Youth Offending Team.

Local authorities have a duty to formulate and implement a written policy on reviews and provide the following people with a copy: the child (unless not appropriate); the parents; any other person with parental responsibility; and any other person considered to be relevant. The policy should ensure a system which provides for a structured and co-ordinated approach to the conduct of reviews, and the full participation, where possible and appropriate, of the child, the parents and the child's carers; the participation of the latter being subject to the wishes and feelings of the child if old enough.

Timing of reviews

Where a looked after child is subject to a child protection plan, a single planning and reviewing process, led by the IRO, should meet the requirements of the 2010 Regulations, the guidance on case reviews (HM Government, 2010) and *Working Together to Safeguard Children* (HM Government, 2013). The timing of child protection review conferences should be planned to be the same as looked after children (LAC) reviews 'to ensure that information in relation to the child's safety is considered within the review meeting, and informs the overall care planning process' (HM Government, 2010:4.10). Consideration also has to be given to ensuring that the multi-agency contribution to the review of the child protection plan is addressed within the review of the care plan.

The maximum interval between reviews is prescribed in reg. 33:

- the first within 20 days of the child becoming looked after;
- the second within three months of the first; and
- the third and subsequent reviews at six-monthly intervals.

> The specified frequency of reviews is a minimum standard. A review should take place as often as the circumstances of the individual case require. (HM Government, 2010:4.6)

Where there is a need for significant change to a care plan, a review should be brought forward and, unless it is not reasonably practicable, no significant change to a care plan should be made unless it has first been considered at a review.

Matters to be considered at reviews

The full details of the many aspects of the child's life which must be considered at each review are set out in Schedule 7 to the 2010 Regulations and elaborated in the guidance (HM Government, 2010: 4.27). They include:

- the effect of any change in the child's circumstances since the last review, particularly of any change to the care plan;

- whether decisions taken at the last review have been successfully implemented and the reasons, if they have not;
- whether any change in the child's legal status should be sought (see, for instance, the key case analysis (*A and S (Children) v Lancashire County Council* [2012]) below (at page 102);
- whether the child has a plan for permanence;
- existing arrangements for contact between the child and others and whether any changes to these arrangements are needed;
- the extent to which the child's placement is the most appropriate available or any changes need to be made before the next review;
- the child's educational needs and the extent to which these are being met or changes to educational arrangements that need to be made before the next review;
- the child's leisure interests;
- the child's health, according to the most recent assessment (reg. 8) and any need to change arrangements for his health care before the next assessment;
- the extent to which the child's identity needs are being met and any change that is required;
- whether the arrangements in regard to an independent visitor for the child continue to be appropriate and she understands how to seek appropriate advice, assistance and support (reg. 31);
- whether any arrangements need to be made for the time when the child ceases to be looked after;
- the child's wishes and feelings and the views of the IRO about any aspect of the case and, in particular, any changes the authority has made or proposes to make to the child's care plan;
- where the child has been placed with a person defined as 'P' under reg. 2 without an assessment of the suitability of the placement being completed, whether the frequency of the local authority representative's visits need any change.

A process should be in place to ensure that information about the child's progress is collected on a continuous basis. Prior to the review, the local authority has to consult widely and take into account the wishes and feelings of the following regarding the care plan and the progress made since the last review:

- the child, subject to age and understanding;
- the birth parents and anyone else with parental responsibility; and

- any other person thought to be relevant, including: foster carers or residential social workers; health care professionals; a representative of any other authority where the child is or may be placed, their officer with lead responsibility for promoting the educational achievement of looked after children; the most appropriate teacher at the child's current or new school (preferably the designated teacher for looked after children); and, if appointed, the independent visitor. (HM Government, 2010:4.17, and see page 69)

Written reports, submitted to the IRO in time to be circulated in advance to all parties due to attend the review, rather than actual attendance, may be considered adequate.

Attendance at the review meeting

It is the responsibility of the child's social worker to prepare her for the review meeting. At least 20 working days before the meeting, the child should be consulted regarding the people she would like to attend the meeting, the venue, and whether she needs to be accompanied by an advocate. This conversation should inform discussions between the social worker and the IRO before invitations to the meeting are sent out. Parents and the child's carers should also be consulted regarding the timing and venue, and parents should, if necessary, be supported with financial or other support so that they can attend. Priority in regard to timing and venue should be given to the needs of the child, who should not have to miss school or health appointments in order to attend.

Children have expressed very clear views about the number of people attending reviews:

> We want to change the way reviews are done. I mean it's your home, you don't want a load of random strangers sitting in your front room. (Voice for the Child in Care, 2004:51)

There are cases in which, in exceptional circumstances, the social worker, having consulted with the IRO, may decide that the child or parent – having consulted with the child – may not attend.

The role of the IRO

The increased responsibilities of IROs under the 2010 Regulations and guidance (DCSF, 2010c) are significant:

The 2008 Act extends the IRO's responsibilities from monitoring the performance by the local authority in relation to a child's **review** to monitoring the performance by the local authority of their functions in relation to a child's **case**, as set out in sections 25A–25C of the 1989 Act (inserted by section 10 of the 2008 Act). The intention is that these changes will enable the IRO to have an effective independent oversight of the child's case and ensure that the child's interests are protected throughout the care planning process.

DCSF, 2010c:1.18

The duties of the IRO are set out in s. 25B Children Act 1989:

s. 25B

(1) The independent reviewing officer must—
 (a) monitor the performance by the local authority of their functions in relation to the child's case;
 (b) participate, in accordance with regulations made by the appropriate national authority, in any review of the child's case;
 (c) ensure that any ascertained wishes and feelings of the child concerning the case are given due consideration by the local authority;
 (d) perform any other function which is prescribed in regulations made by the appropriate national authority.

Children Act 1989

It is the responsibility of the IRO to chair the review meetings of all looked after children.

Reviewing must be understood as a flexible process that will vary in relation to each child. It may be one standalone meeting attended by all the relevant people in the child's life, or a number of meetings with one central meeting attended by the IRO, the child, the social worker and some of the relevant adults in the child's life. It will be for the IRO and the social worker, in consultation with the child, to agree the best way to manage the process for each child before each review.

DCSF, 2010c:3.6

A child-centred meeting

Paragraphs 3.8–22 provide detailed good practice guidance on engaging the child and the parents in the review process, including consideration of flexible arrangements where direct engagement may not be in the child's interests. More specific guidance on ensuring that the review is a child-centred meeting is provided in paras 3.29–37. A review of children's perceptions of their involvement in child safeguarding processes, *Young Views and Voices*, undertaken by the Norfolk Safeguarding Children Board in 2012, suggests that the level of sensitive preparation of the child for reviews is key to their feeling listened to and understanding what is happening in their lives.

> I felt frightened but got more confident – it would have helped if they had prepared me a bit more. (Biswas et al., 2012:3.7)

Issues to be addressed at each review

As chair, the IRO is responsible for ensuring that all the issues set out in Schedule 7 of the 2010 Regulations (see above at page 97) are addressed as part of each review process.

As Jackson J identified in *A and S (Children) v Lancashire County Council* [2012] (see below): 'These are detailed responsibilities. To carry them out properly needs time and care.' (at 195)

Following from a review

After a review, the local authority has to follow its arrangements for implementing decisions made during or as a result of the review, which must include a process for informing the IRO of any failure to implement decisions within an agreed timescale. When the care plan is revised, the local authority must give a copy of the revised plan to the child, the parent(s) and the IRO, and also the person with whom the child is living (HM Government, 2010:4.30).

It is the responsibility of the IRO to complete a written record of each review (reg. 38 2010 Regulations and paras 4.31–33 of the guidance (HM Government, 2010). The record must be placed on the child's case file. It should include:

- an assessment of the extent to which the care plan is meeting the needs of the child;
- in the light of information presented at the review, the identification of changes needed and the outcomes intended;

- a list of decisions made, with the name of the person responsible for implementing them, and relevant timescales.

Access to the representation and complaints procedure and CAFCASS

Differences of opinion arising in the course of a review should, where possible, be resolved on an informal basis. Where they cannot be resolved informally, the local authority should ensure that the child, parents, carers and others involved with the child are aware of the representations procedure the local authority must have in place (s. 26 Children Act 1989 and the Children Act 1989 Representations Procedure (England) Regulations 2006) (see above, pages 70–71). The IRO is under a duty to advise the child of her right to make a complaint and of the availability of an advocate to assist her.

Under s. 25B(3) Children Act 1989, the IRO has the power to refer a case to CAFCASS. This is, however, very much a last resort to be invoked where addressing the IRO's concerns about the plan for the child or the service that is being provided to her cannot be resolved through discussion, use of the complaints procedure, or application to the court for an order under the 1989 Act, either by the child or an adult prepared to act on her behalf. In any event, the 2010 Regulations require that before there is a referral to CAFCASS, the IRO must make 'persons at an appropriate level of seniority within the responsible authority' aware of his concerns and allow them to be addressed 'within a reasonable period of time' (reg. 45(3)(b)). As we have already seen (see page 95) only an infinitesimal number of cases are referred to CAFCASS by IROs.

Pressures on the IRO service

The need for IRO's to have access to independent legal advice is exemplified by the case below. Children the subject of freeing orders under the Adoption Act 1976 were legally cut off from their birth families and, since they were no longer the subject of care orders, without anyone with parental responsibility for them. Although freeing orders were replaced by placement orders under s. 21 Adoption and Children Act 2002 in 2004, those in existence had to be revoked to remove freed children from what has been described as 'legal limbo' (Ball, 2003:20). Ensuring that this happened in a timely way should have been regarded both as being a crucial element of an IRO's responsibilities and a matter where timely legal advice would be essential.

> **KEY CASE ANALYSIS**

A and S (Children) v Lancashire County Council [2012]

A and S were born in 1995 and 1997 and care orders to Lancashire County Council were made in 1998. After an initial kinship placement broke down the boys went into foster care. In 2001, on the authority's application, they were freed for adoption. All contact, with the birth family stopped.

In 2001/2002, the boys spent nine months with abusive foster carers from whom they were removed. In July 2002, they were placed with foster carers Mr and Mrs B and achieved some stability.

In March 2004, the authority formally abandoned the plan for adoption. However, it never applied to revoke the freeing orders, which remained in place.

In February 2008, the placement with Mr and Mrs B ended and in July 2008 the boys moved to live with Mr and Mrs SG. In June 2010, S's behaviour became too much for the SGs to manage and in October 2010 he was placed in a children's home and in February 2011 he moved to another one.

Between 1999 and 2011, each boy was the subject of 35 LAC reviews. From March 2004, every LAC review recommended that the freeing orders ought to be revoked on an application by the authority. The LAC reviews also gave recommendations and advice about contact. During an LAC review in 2006, the boys specifically asked to be allowed to see their brothers and the social worker agreed to discuss whether direct contact could take place. However, there was no record of that being followed up.

At age 16, A had had 12 main placements and had been in respite care 36 times, with 19 different respite carers. At age 14, S had had 16 main placements and had been in respite care 40 times, with at least 22 different respite carers.

A and S brought proceedings under the Human Rights Act 1998 against the authority and its employee, the IRO.

The authority and the IRO accepted that they had breached the boys' rights under the ECHR and gave explanations of the failings which had occurred. The Children's Guardian gave evidence that both S and A were profoundly damaged by their journey through the care system.

It was held had the boys been under a care order, the authority would have been obliged to permit and promote reasonable contact with their mother and siblings in accordance with their statutory obligations to a child in care under s. 34(1) and Schedule 2, para.

15(1) Children Act 1989. Further, the failure to revoke the freeing order had amounted to a denial of access to the court process and had deprived the children, *inter alia*, of the protection and scrutiny of having a Children's Guardian appointed for them. In the circumstances, the authority and the IRO had acted incompatibly with the rights of A and S as guaranteed by Articles 8, 6 and 3 ECHR. The judgment also lists other critical failures of Lancashire County Council and the IRO.

Peter Jackson J suggested that the IRO's evidence went a long way to explain the utter ineffectiveness of the independent reviewing system in protecting A and S's interests (see [117], [122], [124]–[126], [146] of the judgment).

A and S were awarded damages for breach of statutory duty. *Per curiam*:

> IROs need to have sufficient training and experience to recognise the importance of issues of the kind raised by A and S's case. These were children with increasingly complex needs, but there is no record of any serious consideration being given to important questions such as whether keeping them together was in their interests, nor any acknowledgement of the possible value and purpose of family contact ... All that can be said is that there is an obligation on every local authority to ensure that IROs have access to legal advice. ([200], [209])

The evidence of the IRO, who fully acknowledged his culpability in failing to safeguard the children, provides a detailed commentary on: the complexity of the role; the impact of a caseload of more than three times that recommended in guidance; and other pressures on individuals in the system. Early findings from research being undertaken by the National Children's Bureau (NCB) into the role of the IRO in improving care planning for looked after children, presented to the National Association of Independent Reviewing Officers (NAIRO) conference in September 2012, suggest that his may not have been an isolated experience. Whilst acknowledging that in many authorities the service is supported to function effectively, concerns have been raised in a letter to the Minister for Children by the NAIRO regarding the intimidation of IROs by managers in some local authorities (www.nairo.org.uk).

In their commentary on the *Lancashire* case, Knowles and Sharp (2012) reflect critically on the Family Justice Review's failure – having referred to 'often ill founded' but widespread distrust of local authorities' ability and willingness to implement a care plan in the best interests of the child, and associated concerns about the independence of IROs and their heavy workload – to analyse why IROs were perceived to be ineffective advocates for children or to evidence its belief that IROs could effectively influence care planning.

Concerns about the delays in achieving permanence, placement instability and poor outcomes for looked after children and the reliance placed on the IRO to resolve these problems have been voiced for a long time (DfES, 2006; 2007). In a critical commentary, Thomas (2011) suggests that in the area of planning and reviews for looked after children, research has failed over more than a decade to keep pace with changes in policy and practice. He reports the lack of substantial studies of planning and reviewing since late in the last century, and the fact that there were none into the work of IROs.

In contrast, Thomas identified several studies canvassing the views of children and young people about their involvement in the planning and review process (Voice for the Child in Care, 2004; Morgan, 2006; Timms and Thoburn, 2006). The findings of these studies were largely replicated in those of the recent review of children's perceptions of their involvement in child safeguarding processes, *Young Views and Voices*, referred to above (Biswas et al., 2012). The findings from all these studies suggest that the level of sensitive preparation of children and young people for reviews, and help in expressing their views, is key to their feeling listened to and understanding what is happening in their lives.

The dearth of research evidence regarding the different ways in which the service is managed within local authorities and its effectiveness should soon be remedied. In addition to the ongoing NCB study referred to above, the Centre for Research into the Child and the Family at the University of East Anglia is undertaking a major investigation of care planning and the role of the IRO. When completed, these two studies should substantially improve understanding of the effectiveness of the IRO service and identify barriers to its efficacy in achieving better outcomes for looked after children.

Further reading

Department for Children, Schools and Families (2010c) *IRO Handbook*, to which reference is made throughout this chapter, provides detailed guidance on all aspects of the role and responsibilities of IROs. It repays detailed study rather than casual reference.

National Association of Independent Reviewing Officers www.nairo.org.uk. This website is a useful source of commentary on developments and current concerns for the service.

Research studies: findings from the ongoing research studies referred to above are likely to be published in due course in journals such as: *British Journal of Social Work, Child and Family Law Quarterly, Child and Family Social Work* and the *Journal of Social Welfare and Family Law*.

8

ALTERNATIVE LEGAL ARRANGEMENTS

The range of arrangements

The Children Act 1989 introduced a greater flexibility into the legal arrangements that can be made for children unable to live with their own families, either on a temporary or permanent basis. Under earlier legislation, the sharp divide between orders made in private and public law proceedings prevented courts in the latter from reaching sensible legal solutions, not involving public care, for children needing a permanent placement outside their birth family (see, for instance, Ball, 1990). On implementation of the Act, the range of orders available to resolve differences about the upbringing of their children between parents following divorce was increased, and some of these orders also became available to courts in care proceedings and to provide statutory remedies instead of resort to the **wardship** jurisdiction of the High Court. This flexibility was increased further when the new legal concept of special guardianship was enacted as an amendment to the 1989 Act by the Adoption and Children Act 2002.

As an alternative to being looked after, children may achieve permanence outside the public care system through child arrangements orders (s. 8 Children Act 1989) or special guardianship (ss 14A–G). Additionally, without the formality of a court order though subject to regulation, children living under a variety of informal arrangements come within the definition of being privately fostered. Outside the scope of this book, at the most extreme end of the permanence spectrum, a child may be adopted, thus effecting the legal transfer of the child to the adoptive family, with irrevocable legal severance from the birth family.

Child arrangements orders

When part 2 of the Children and Families Act 2014 comes into force, residence and contact orders will be replaced by child arrangements orders.

s. 12 Child arrangements orders

(1) Section 8(1) of the Children Act 1989 is amended as follows.
(2) Omit the definitions of 'contact order' and 'residence order'.
(3) After 'In this Act—' insert—
   'child arrangements order' means an order regulating arrangements relating to any of the following—

    (a) with whom a child is to live, spend time or otherwise have contact, and

    (b) when a child is to live, spend time or otherwise have contact with any person;'.

(4) Schedule 2 (amendments relating to child arrangements orders) has effect.

Children and Families Act 2014

Residence orders are currently one of a suite of private law orders: residence, contact, prohibited steps and specific issues which may be made under s. 8 Children Act 1989. The change to a child arrangements order, which enacts a recommendation in the Family Justice Review, is put in context in Supreme Court Justice Lady Hale's submission to that review:

> The thinking behind the Children Act 1989 was that parents should be encouraged to make their own arrangements and the court would only decide what they could not decide. But their task, and the court's task, was not to allocate status or rights, so much as to settle the practical living arrangements for the child. Over the years, 'residence' and 'contact' have taken on too much of the flavour of the old 'custody' and 'access' orders. These proposals would restore the original vision underlying the 1989 Act.
>
> *Family Justice Review Panel, 2011:4.65*

Although private law orders are primarily sought following the breakdown of the parents' relationship, such was the flexibility introduced by the 1989 Act that child arrangements orders, limited to arrangements as to with whom the child will live (Schedule 2, Part 2, para. 4(6B)), may, subject to the welfare test in s. 1 of the Act, be made by courts in public law proceedings. Child arrangements orders may be applied for as of right or with leave of the court. Details as to those who may apply as of right or only with leave of the court are set out in s. 10 Children Act 1989.

    Applications as of right may be made by:

- parents, guardians or special guardians;
- **step-parents** with parental responsibility (s. 4A Children Act 1989);
- a party to marriage (whether or not subsisting) in relation to whom the child has been a **child of the family**;

- a partner in a **civil partnership** (whether or not subsisting) in relation to whom the child has been a child of the family;
- any person with whom the child has lived for at least three years (not necessarily continuously but must be within the previous five years and not have ended more than three months before the application);
- any person '(i) in any case where the residence element of a child arrangements order is in force with respect to the child, has the consent of each of the persons in whose favour the order was made; (ii) in any case where the child is in the care of a local authority, has the consent of that authority; or (iii) in any other case, has the consent of each of those (if any) who have parental responsibility for the child' (s. 10(5)(c));
- a relative of the child, if the child has lived with her for at least one year immediately preceding the application;
- a foster parent with whom the child has lived for at least a year immediately preceding the application.

Applications with leave

A child may be granted leave to apply if the court is satisfied he has sufficient understanding to make the application. All others seeking a child arrangements order can only do so with leave of the court. When considering whether to grant leave, the court will pay particular regard to:

- the applicant's connection with the child;
- any risk there might be of that proposed application disrupting the child's life to such an extent that he would be harmed by it; and
- where the child is being looked after by a local authority, the authority's plans for the child's future; and the wishes and feelings of the child's parents.

It should be noted that where a special guardianship order is in place (see page 115), applications by all those normally able to apply as of right can only be made with leave of the court (s. 10(7A)). Also, a local authority foster parent, or anyone who has been a foster parent within the last six months, may not apply for leave if the child has lived with him for less than a year, unless he is a relative of the child or has the consent of the local authority (s. 9(3)).

A child arrangements order, which will, if not revoked earlier, last until the child is 18, gives the person(s) with whom the child lives limited parental responsibility for the child for the duration of the order. This limited parental responsibility does not allow the holder to appoint a guardian for the child in the event of the holder's death or allow him to consent to the child's adoption, or change the child's name or religion.

Because of these limitations, if a father without parental responsibility applies for a child arrangements order, the court making the order will at the same time make a parental responsibility order under s. 4. This will equate his position with that of the birth mother, except that he, as holder of the child arrangements order, will be able to determine where the child will live.

When a child arrangements order is in place no one may cause the child to be known by a new surname, or remove her from the UK for more than a month without the written consent of everyone who has parental responsibility or leave of the court (s. 13 Children Act 1989).

A child arrangements order can provide a child with the security of a permanent placement without the involvement of the local authority. However, in some cases, where the criteria for making a care order under s. 31(2) are satisfied, a court may make a child arrangements order with a supervision order to the local authority (s. 35 and Schedule 3 Children Act 1989) at the same time, rather than a care order. The decision will rest on issues as to Article 8 ECHR proportionality dependent on the facts of each case. The factors determining 'whether the level of protection which can be offered to the child under a supervision order will be adequate or whether it is necessary to go further and make a full care order' are best explored through the case law (see, for instance, Bainham and Gilmore, 2013:628–31).

The problem with child arrangements orders is that parents and others entitled to apply as of right for revocation or variation of the order may continue to do so, thus subjecting the child's carers to stressful, sometimes vexatious, litigation and putting the security of the arrangement in doubt. Although the 1989 Act does provide the means under s. 91(14) for courts to prevent named individuals making applications under s. 8 without leave, the courts have been cautious in using this power, especially when it concerns parents. If, however, the principles set out in *Re P (Section 91(14) Guidelines) (Residence and Religious Heritage)* [1999] are satisfied, they will do so (*Re M (Parental Responsibility Order)* [2013]).

> **KEY CASE ANALYSIS**

Re D (Care or Supervision Order) [2000]

The unmarried mother of a six-year-old boy was an alcoholic. The child was removed from her care and placed with the father, with whom she had a parental responsibility agreement. In conjoined public and private law proceedings, the question arose of what orders to make. The local authority sought a supervision order and supported a residence order in favour of the father. The guardian ad litem argued for a care order with the child placed with the father.

It was held that making a supervision order for 12 months in favour of the local authority and a residence order in favour of the father:

(1) If the balance between a care order and a supervision order is equal, the court should adopt the least interventionist approach. The court should ask itself whether:
    (a) the stronger order is needed to protect the child;
    (b) the risks could be met by a supervision order;
    (c) there is a need for the sort of speed of action that a care order gives a local authority;
    (d) the father could protect the child without sharing parental responsibility with the authority;
    (e) parental co-operation could only be obtained through the more draconian order;
    (f) the child's needs could be met by advising, assisting and befriending him rather than by sharing parental responsibility of him;
    (g) there have been any improvements seen by objective observers during the current proceedings which would indicate the future, and the range of powers allotted to a supervision order, including its duration.
(2) courts should not saddle local authorities with care orders if it really is not necessary to do so, when they have so many demands on their resources.

On-the-spot question	Where the s. 31 criteria for making a care order are satisfied, what human rights issues will a court have to consider in deciding whether to make a care order or a child arrangements and supervision order?

Special guardianship

The rationale for the introduction of the new legal concept of special guardianship was spelt out in the White Paper *Adoption: A New Approach*:

> Adoption is not always appropriate for children who cannot return to their birth parents. Some older children do not wish to be legally separated from their birth families. Adoption may not be best for some children being cared for on a permanent basis by members of their wider birth family. Some minority ethnic communities have religious and cultural difficulties with adoption as it is set out in law. Unaccompanied asylum seeking children may also need secure permanent homes, but have strong attachments to their families abroad. All these children deserve the same chance as any other to enjoy the benefits of a legally secure, stable permanent placement that promotes a supportive, lifelong relationship with their carers, where the court decides that it is in their best interests.
>
> *DH, 2000:5.8*

The White Paper proposals were enacted in the Adoption and Children Act 2002 to introduce ss 14A–G into the 1989 Act.

Eligibility to apply for special guardianship

A special guardianship order may be made on the application of a person or persons entitled to apply, or with leave of the court. The applicant must be aged 18 or over and must not be a parent of the child. As with child arrangements orders, a person who is, or was at any time within the last six months, a local authority foster parent of a child may not apply for leave unless he has the consent of the authority, is a relative of the child, or the child has lived with him for at least one year preceding the application (s. 9(3) Children Act 1989).

Applications as of right may be made by those listed in s. 14A(5), or a court may make a special guardianship order with respect to a child in any family proceedings in which a question arises with respect to the welfare of the child, if an application for the order has been made by an individual entitled to apply, or more than one such individual jointly, or the court considers that a special guardianship order should be made even though no application has been made (in which case there will have to be an adjournment for preparation of the report referred to below).

Use of special guardianship

The special guardianship provisions span private and public law. They are located with private law orders in Part II Children Act 1989 and subject to that Act's welfare checklist. However, the White Paper (DH, 2000) made it clear that the order is intended to provide an alternative to adoption for looked after children in care. As such, although a private law order, it forms part of the state's child protection provision, with social workers playing a key role in preparing the court report on the suitability of the applicant to become a special guardian. Through the Special Guardianship Regulations 2005, it is as highly regulated as adoption and fostering and attracts similar support services, including financial support (Special Guardianship Regulations 2005, regs 6–10).

When the special guardianship provisions came into force in 2005, there was initially some confusion as to the existence of any presumption as to whether in any particular category of case adoption was preferable to special guardianship. In the Court of Appeal, Wall LJ gave helpful guidance, emphasizing that in each case the decision should depend on its particular facts.

> **KEY CASE ANALYSIS**

Re S (A Child) (Adoption Order or Special Guardianship Order) [2007]

S, aged seven, was in care and had lived with her foster carer for most of her life. The local authority's plan was for S to be adopted and her foster carer applied to adopt her. S's mother sought discharge of the care order and contact. The judge at first instance decided that S should live with her foster carer under a special guardianship order. The decision not to make an adoption order was appealed.

When dismissing the appeal, Wall LJ considered the underlying principles to be applied in making adoption or special guardianship orders and gave guidance to courts of first instance on the proper approach in such cases.

> [I]n addition to the fundamental difference in status between adopted children and those subject to special guardianship

orders, there are equally fundamental differences between the status and powers of adopters and special guardians. These, we think, need to be borne in mind when the court is applying the welfare checklist under both section 1(3)(a) of the 1989 Act and section 1 of the 2002 Act.

Certain other points arise from the statutory scheme:—

(i) The carefully constructed statutory regime (notice to the local authority, leave requirements in certain cases, the role of the court, and the report from the local authority—even where the order is made by the court of its own motion) demonstrates the care which is required before making a special guardianship order, and that it is only appropriate if, in the particular circumstances of the particular case, it is best fitted to meet the needs of the child or children concerned.

(ii) There is nothing in the statutory provisions themselves which limits the making of a special guardianship order or an adoption order to any given set of circumstances. The statute itself is silent on the circumstances in which a special guardianship order is likely to be appropriate, and there is no presumption contained within the statute that a special guardianship order is preferable to an adoption order in any particular category of case. Each case must be decided on its particular facts; and each case will involve the careful application of a judicial discretion to those facts.

(iii) The key question which the court will be obliged to ask itself in every case in which the question of adoption as opposed to special guardianship arises will be: which order will better serve the welfare of this particular child? ([46]–[47])

In a later case, the Court of Appeal emphasized the need for special guardianship rather than adoption to be considered whenever the child's welfare might require it.

After a slow start the number of special guardianship orders made in all courts in private and public law proceedings has risen steadily to 1921 in 2011. The role of special guardianship in permanency planning has been helpfully reviewed by the BAAF (Simmonds, 2011).

> → **KEY CASE ANALYSIS** ←

Re I (Adoption: Appeal: Special Guardianship) [2012]

The father and paternal grandmother applied for permission to appeal against an order dispensing with the father's consent to placement for adoption of the child, who had been in foster care since she had been discharged from hospital following her premature birth in 2007. It was envisaged that the foster carers would adopt her but that the regular contact she had with the father and paternal grandmother should continue. No order for contact was made.

Granting leave to appeal, it was held that:

1 The issue for the judge had been narrowly but importantly to determine the legal status that the child would have in the care of the foster carers. It was therefore surprising that very little reference was made to the option of special guardianship. The distinction between special guardianship and adoption should have been uppermost in the court's consideration given that the paternal natural family would continue to play a meaningful part in the child's life.

2 It was not possible for the judge to have decided that the welfare of the child 'required' adoption under s. 52 unless he had given active and detailed consideration to the pros and cons of special guardianship as an alternative disposal.

The effect of special guardianship orders

The main effect of the order is to confer parental responsibility on the special guardian(s), which may then be exercised to the exclusion of any other person. Although the order may be varied or discharged on the application of any of the persons specified in s. 14D Children Act 1989, in order to protect special guardians from litigation which might disrupt their parenting role, all applicants except the local authority require leave to make an application. Except in regard to the child, leave will only be granted if the court is satisfied that there has been a 'significant change' in circumstances since the order was made (s. 14D(5)). However, the Court of Appeal, in *Re G (A Child) (Special Guardianship Order: Application to Discharge)* [2010], noted that the requirement that the change be 'significant' did not appear in other provisions of the 1989 Act relating to leave. The court determined that, in the interests of simplicity, the same approach should be adopted in relation to applications to discharge special guardianship orders as applied in relation to the discharge of placement orders (s. 24 Adoption and Children Act 2002), following the approach recommended in *Re M (Children) (Placement Order)* [2007].

On-the-spot questions

1 When a child cannot live with her parent(s), what alternative private law legal arrangements may be made?
2 How does special guardianship differ from adoption?

Private fostering

A child is privately fostered if under 16 (18 if disabled) and cared for and accommodated by someone other than a parent, someone with parental responsibility, or a close relative. The definition excludes children looked after in this way for less than 28 days when it is not intended that the arrangement should last for longer. The essence of a private fostering arrangement is that is made privately, without the involvement of the local authority. Put starkly:

> Parents require a service, foster carers offer a service—the two sides contact each other, negotiate the terms and the goods (the children) change hands. (Holman, 1973:10)

Privately fostered children include children placed with strangers for lengthy periods, often while their parents pursue studies, have work commitments or live overseas; adolescents who are temporarily estranged from their families; children who attend language schools and independent schools in the UK; children from abroad on more than 27-day holiday or exchange visits; children who are asylum seekers; and some children brought to the UK from overseas with a view to adoption; a considerably wider range than a literal reading of Holman's comment might suggest.

Policy context

Private fostering arrangements have been described as 'among the least controlled and most open to abuse of all the environments in which children live away from home' (Utting, 1997). A description chillingly exemplified in the torture leading to her death from hypothermia and starvation suffered by Victoria Climbié at the hands of her great-aunt, by whom she was privately fostered, and her partner. Lord Laming's inquiry into Victoria's death called for greater regulation of private fostering but developments so far have, despite amendments to Part IX and Schedule 8 Children Act 1989 introduced by the Children Act 2004, fallen short of the inquiry's recommendations (Laming, 2003:17.12–14).

As the guidance (DfES, 2005a:1.7) recognizes: 'privately fostered children remain a diverse and potentially vulnerable group'; the largest percentage being West African children (Philpot, 2001). Although many local authorities make considerable efforts to encourage the reporting of private fostering arrangements, there is general recognition that the number of notifications is much lower than the actual incidence (www. privatefostering.org.uk). This means that it is likely that many privately fostered children are left without the protection afforded by local authority scrutiny of the suitability of the arrangement to safeguard their welfare. There is a wide discrepancy between rates of reporting across authorities.

PRACTICE FOCUS

Ellie is five years old. She is known as Ellie Smith and has a seven-year-old 'sister' who also attends the local school. Ms Smith explained to the school nurse that Ellie's mother is a friend of hers and has gone abroad for work. Ms Smith says she agreed to care for Ellie until her mother is able to return to the UK.

The nurse realizes that this is a private fostering arrangement and asks Ms Smith whether the local authority is offering any help and advice. Ms Smith informs her that there is no need for their involvement as this is strictly between herself and Ellie's mother. The nurse tells Ms Smith that because this is a private fostering arrangement she must inform the local authority, and gives her the contact details of the local children's services office. She also talks to her about how they might be able to assist. Ms Smith appears taken aback and non-committal about getting in touch with the local authority.

When the nurse talks to Ms Smith some time later she realizes that she has not been in touch with the local authority. The nurse explains that she has a responsibility to inform the local authority and asks permission to do so. Ms Smith becomes quite aggressive and tells the nurse that this is none of her business. The nurse talks to her and Ellie about what has to be done, trying to reassure them that she will be acting in Ellie's interests.

• Should the nurse take any further action?

The thrust of policy developments and legislation has been to regulate in order to safeguard and promote the welfare of privately fostered children, through basic scrutiny of the suitability of arrangements before they begin and review of the child's situation throughout the arrangement.

Notification scheme

Enacting many of the recommendations of the inquiry into the death of Victoria Climbié, ss 44–47 Children Act 2004 and the Children (Private Arrangements for Fostering) Regulations 2005 amended the law on private fostering arrangements and the role of the local authority. The Act provides for a notification scheme, which has been in place since 2005, and for a registration scheme, long called for by many commentators and all leading child care organizations (Philpot, 2001). There is a time-limited power to introduce a registration scheme, but it has not yet been implemented, and there is no sign of political will to bring this about.

Responsibilities of the local authority, parents and private foster carers

Published to coincide with implementation of the revised regulation of private fostering, introduced through amendment of the Children Act 1989 by the Children Act 2004, *The Replacement Children Act 1989 Guidance on Private Fostering* (DfES, 2005a) provides practice guidance in this difficult area, underpinned by national standards (DfES, 2005b). The effect is to extend the responsibility of the local authority to raise awareness of the need for notification (Schedule 8, para. 7A Children Act 1989) and to satisfy itself as to the suitability of proposed private fostering as well as to monitor existing arrangements, and to offer such advice as it thinks necessary in regard to proposed as well as existing arrangements (s. 67(1) Children Act 1989). Local authorities' performance against the regulations and NMS are inspected by Ofsted.

The guidance (DfES, 2005a) identifies the relevant responsibilities between the private foster carer, the parent or person with parental responsibility and the local authority:

- the private foster carer is responsible for providing day-to-day care in a way which will safeguard and promote the child's welfare;

- the parent or other person with parental responsibility has overarching responsibility for safeguarding and promoting the child's welfare; and
- it is the duty of the local authority to satisfy itself that the welfare of children who are or will be privately fostered is being or will be adequately safeguarded or promoted.

Where the agreement is a private one made between the parents and carers, the arrangement is one of private fostering and the child is not a looked after child. These cases need to be distinguished from circumstances in which the local authority, with the consent of the parents, has become involved in the arrangements, in which case the child is legally defined as being accommodated under s. 20, and is a 'looked after child'.

Notification

The Children (Private Arrangements for Fostering) Regulations 2005 provide minute details of the information required on notification of a forthcoming arrangement (at reg. 3 and Schedule 1). This is fleshed out in para. 2.17 of the guidance (DfES, 2005a), as is the action to be taken by the local authority when notified. Failure by a private foster carer to allow the local authority to exercise its duty, or to comply with a disqualification under s. 68 and the Disqualification from Caring for Children (England) Regulations 2002 or Disqualification from Caring for Children (Wales) Regulations 2004 may result in criminal proceedings.

On-the-spot questions	1 Why is there a need for private fostering arrangements to be regulated? 2 How could current regulation be made more effective?

Further reading

British Association for Adoption and Fostering: www.privatefostering.org.uk – this is a well-designed informative website hosted by BAAF.

Probert, R (2012) *Cretney and Probert's Family Law.* Chapters 13 and 14 of this student textbook provide a clear account of private and public law orders relating to children.

Simmonds, J (2011) *The Role of Special Guardianship in Permanency Planning for Children in England and Wales.* This book helpfully reviews the case law and research evidence regarding the place of special guardianship in permanency planning for looked after children.

Philpot, T (2001) *A Very Private Practice: An Investigation into Private Fostering.* A very readable exploration of the extent and potential for abuse in private fostering arrangements.

9

LOOKED AFTER CHILDREN'S TRANSITION TO ADULTHOOD

AT A GLANCE THIS CHAPTER COVERS:

- the policy context of local authorities' current responsibilities towards children who have been looked after
- the distinctions between different categories of care leavers
- the levels of support for the different categories
- personal advisers and pathway plans
- care leavers with additional needs

Informed by research, since the 1980s the thrust of policy and legislation has been increasingly to recognize the vulnerability of young care leavers and to seek to regulate, as far as is possible, for a successful transition to adulthood. The recent social context being the decline in the youth labour market, the growth of education and training, the shortage of affordable housing for young people and a welfare benefits system which discourages young people from leaving home. As a result '[p]athways to adulthood for most young people have become more differentiated and challenging over recent decades' (Wade and Dixon, 2006:199).

The implications of these realities for young care leavers are recognized in the aspirational rationale for the current legal framework set out in statutory guidance:

Transition to adulthood is often a turbulent time: transitions are no longer always sequential – leave school, work, relationship, setting up home, parenthood. Young people can become adult in one area but not in others. For many young adults, their transition to adulthood can be extended and delayed until they are emotionally and financially ready and they have the qualifications they need and aspire to, so that they have the opportunity to achieve their economic potential. Young people from care may not have this option. Whilst most young people know they can call on the support of their families to help them through unforeseen difficulties, care leavers may not be able to rely on unqualified support if things do not work out as they make their journey into adulthood.

Care leavers should expect the same level of care and support that others would expect from a reasonable parent. The local authority responsible for their care should make sure that they are provided with the opportunities they need, which will include offering them more than one chance as they grapple with taking on the responsibilities of adulthood.

DfE, 2010b:1.7 and 1.8

Consistent research findings, both national and international, show that a majority of young people leaving care make the transition to adulthood between the ages of 16 and 18, whereas many of their peers do not do so until their mid-twenties. Children leaving care are also more likely than other young people to:

- have poorer educational qualifications;
- have lower levels of participation in further and higher education;
- be young parents;

- be homeless; and
- have higher levels of unemployment, offending behaviour and mental health problems (Stein, 2009b).

However, some young care leavers do make the transition to adulthood successfully. Research identifies remedial factors aiding the transition:

- stable foster placements throughout childhood;
- the ability to remain with foster carers into adulthood or to continue to receive a high level of social care support;
- a strong attachment to at least one adult;
- educational support in school and beyond; and
- active participation in social, leisure and informal learning activities.

All these factors, or a combination of them, are associated with what are identified as 'good outcomes' by both young people and foster carers (Sinclair et al. 2005; Stein, 2009b; Hollingworth, 2012; Jackson, 2013).

The current legal framework governing local authorities' responsibilities towards young people making the transition from being looked after to independent living is enacted in Part III and Schedule 2 Children Act 1989 (most recently amended by the Children and Young Persons Act 2008), Care Planning, Placement and Case Review (England) Regulations 2010 (the Care Planning Regulations) and the Care Leavers (England) Regulations 2010 (the Care Leavers Regulations). This chapter covers the main elements of these responsibilities and those towards groups with special needs such as children with disabilities, UASCs and care leavers in the youth justice system, all of whom require specialist support.

Entitlement to care-leaving support

Various categories of young people are entitled to different levels of support as they make the transition to adulthood.

- *Eligible children*: those aged 16 or 17 who are looked after and have been for a period of 13 weeks, or periods amounting to 13 weeks in total, which began after they were 14 and ended after they reached 16 years (Schedule 2, para. 19B Children Act 1989 and reg. 40 Care Planning Regulations)
- *Relevant children*: (i) those aged 16 or 17 who are not looked after, but who, before they last ceased to be looked after, were eligible children; (ii) those aged 16 or 17, not looked after, and who before they were

detained in a penal institution or hospital had been looked after for a period amounting to at least 13 weeks since the age of 14; (iii) where a child aged 16 or 17 has lived for a continuous period of six months with a parent, someone else with parental responsibility for her, or where she is in care and there was a child arrangements order in force immediately before the care order was made, a person in whose favour the child arrangements order was made, that child is not a relevant child despite falling within s. 23A. However, if any of these arrangements breaks down and the child ceases to live with the person concerned, the child is treated as a relevant child.

- *Former relevant children*: young people who are aged 18 or above and either have been relevant children and would be if they were under 18, or immediately before they ceased to be looked after at age 18, were eligible children.
- *Former relevant children pursuing further education or training:* a former relevant child who is aged under 25, in relation to whom the duties in s. 23C(2), (3) and (4) no longer apply, and she has informed the local authority that she wants to pursue, or is pursuing, a programme of education and training.
- *Persons qualifying for advice and assistance:* under s. 24, the following come in to this category: an individual aged 16 to 20 with respect to whom a special guardianship order is in force, or was when they reached 18, and who was looked after immediately before the making of that order; or at any time after reaching the age of 16 but while he was still under 18, was, but is no longer, looked after, accommodated or fostered.

	Are the following **eligible, relevant** or **former relevant** children?
	1 **Jim**, who is now 17, was made the subject of a care order when he was 14. When he was 15 and six months his foster parents obtained a special guardianship order.
On-the-spot questions	2 **Maria**, who is now 17, was accommodated for six months when she was 13.
	3 **David**, who is now aged 16, has been the subject of a care order since he was 10.
	4 **Julie**, who is now 17, was looked after for three months when she was 14 and again for three months starting when she was nearly 16.

Local authorities' duties to provide care-leaving support

Eligible children

In addition to the obligations that the local authority has to all looked after children (see Chapters 4 and 5), once a looked after child becomes eligible the authority must:

- prepare an assessment of the level of advice, assistance and support it will provide before and after the young person ceases to be looked after (Schedule 2, para. 19B(4), Children Act 1989 and reg. 42 Care Planning Regulations);
- prepare a pathway plan, which includes the care plan, and which adheres to the requirements in reg. 43;
- keep the pathway plan under regular review; and
- appoint a personal adviser for the child, to fulfil the functions set out in reg. 44.

Relevant children

The local authority that last looked after the relevant child must:

- take reasonable steps to keep in touch with the child;
- prepare an assessment of the child's needs with a view to determining what advice, assistance and support it should provide (regs 4 and 5 Care Leavers Regulations);
- prepare a pathway plan following the requirements set out in reg. 6 Care Leavers Regulations;
- keep the pathway plan under regular review;
- appoint a personal adviser, unless one was appointed when the young person was an eligible child, to fulfil the functions in reg. 8 Care Leavers Regulations;
- safeguard and promote the relevant child's welfare by maintaining him, providing him with or maintaining him in suitable accommodation and providing assistance in order to meet his needs in relation to education, training or employment as provided for in the pathway plan (s. 23B(8) Children Act 1989 and reg. 9 Care Leavers Regulations).

Former relevant children

The local authority that last looked after the former relevant child must:

- take reasonable steps to keep in touch with her (s. 23C(2) Children Act 1989), and if necessary re-establish contact;
- continue to keep the pathway plan under regular review;
- continue the appointment of a personal adviser;
- if her welfare requires it, provide financial assistance to allow her to undertake or seek employment; or pursue education or training;
- if a former relevant child pursues higher education in accordance with her pathway plan, pay her the higher education bursary (s. 23C(5A) Children Act 1989 and Children Act 1989 (Higher Education Bursary) (England) Regulations 2009). These duties continue until the child reaches 21 or, where her pathway plan sets out a programme of education extending beyond that, for as long as the programme is pursued.

Former relevant children pursuing education or training

The local authority that owed duties to the former relevant child under s. 23C Children Act 1989 must:

- appoint a personal adviser to carry out the functions specified in reg. 8 Care Leavers Regulations;
- carry out an assessment of the person's needs in order to determine what, if any, assistance it would be appropriate to provide (s. 23CA(3)(a) Children Act 1989 and regs 4 and 5 Care Leavers Regulations);
- prepare a pathway plan (reg. 6 Care Leavers Regulations);
- to the extent that the person's educational or training needs require it, provide financial assistance (s. 23CA(4) and (5) Children Act 1989). The Court of Appeal has held recently that the duty under s. 23C(4) extends to paying the university tuition fees of foreign nationals who are former relevant children (R (Kebede and Another) v Newcastle City Council [2013]) regardless of resource constraints.

Persons qualifying for advice and assistance

The relevant local authority (s. 24(5) Children Act 1989) must consider whether the person needs help of a kind that the local authority can give:

- to advise and befriend and give assistance (s. 24A);
- to give financial assistance (s. 23CA(4) and (5));
- or, where the person is under 25, assistance in regard to vacation accommodation (ss 24A(2) and (3) and 24B).

Chapters 2 and 3 of the guidance *Planning Transition to Adulthood for Care Leavers* (DfE, 2010b) helpfully amplify the complex legal framework and address key practice issues in regard to pathway planning and the support of advisers.

On-the-spot question	Which provisions requiring support for eligible children are aimed at improving their educational opportunities?

Research evidence to inform practice

Research, much of it funded by government, informed the reforms to the Children Act 1989 introduced by the Children (Leaving Care) Act 2000 (Biehal et al., 1995) and the Care Matters agenda enacted in the Children and Young Persons Act 2008 and through amended regulations, and amplified in revised guidance (Stein, 2004; DfE, 2010b).

Care leavers with additional needs

Disabled young people

In addition to their general responsibilities to all care leavers, local authorities have duties to disabled care leavers under the following legislation:

- Disabled Persons Act 1986
- Learning and Skills Act 2000
- Education Act 1996
- Housing Act 1996
- Community Care Act 1996
- Mental Capacity Act 2005
- Equality Act 2010.

Owing to their additional needs the transition to adulthood for disabled care leavers may be complicated by the number of services, each possibly with its own care plan, that the young person draws on. The transition from support by children's services to support from adult health and social care services needs to be carefully managed and the roles and responsibilities of all involved must be discussed with the young person and his carers. As the guidance indicates, the need is for 'person-centred planning' that will ensure that the planning for a disabled young person to make the transition to adulthood is:

focused on what is important to the young person for the future and what needs to be in place to ensure that they receive the support and achieve their goals. The young person must be kept at the centre with family members, carers and friends being partners in supporting the young person to achieve their potential. A shared commitment should be established to ensure that the young person's views are listened to and ways are found to remove any organisational barriers that might limit personal development and choices.

DfE, 2010b:6.5

The guidance emphasizes the need for all agencies to work together with clear understanding of each other's roles, responsibilities, professional boundaries and legal duties within the transition process. This understanding should be underpinned by specific agreements and protocols (6.7–6.10). Although it pre-dates the additional responsibilities of local authorities to all care leavers under the amendments introduced by the Children and Young Persons Act 2008 and the amended regulations (see pages 123–24), *Future Positive*, a resource guide produced in the West of England for people working with disabled care leavers, provides many examples of good practice (DfES and Others, 2006).

The Mental Capacity Act 2005 and its accompanying Code of Practice (Department for Constitutional Affairs, 2007) provide the statutory framework for people who lack the **mental capacity** to make decisions for themselves. It does not apply to children under the age of 15, but it does apply (with specified exceptions) to 16- and 17-year-olds.

UASCs and separated children

The guidance recognizes that planning transition for these children is 'a particularly complex process that needs to address the young people's care needs in the context of wider asylum and immigration legislation and how these needs change over time' (DfE, 2010b:6.20). The complexity is made greater because the majority will have arrived when they are in their mid-teens. This means that there is only a short time in which to both provide for their primary needs – settlement, stability, the opportunity to build new and meaningful attachments and to gain a foothold in education: 'fundamental prerequisites for successful transition at a later stage' – whilst also planning ahead (Wade et al., 2005:183).

Where the young person's entitlement to remain in the UK is uncertain, care planning may realistically need to focus on short-term achievable goals rather than long-term plans. However, pathway planning to support UASCs should still cover all the areas addressed within young people's plans as well as issues arising from their immigration status. In regard to these, Wade et al. offer practical advice learned from the experience of their research cohort:

> Careful monitoring and recording of the progress of young people's asylum applications are critical. Although the progress of claims is effectively outside the control of social work practitioners, up-to-date information about the current state of claims and about what steps need to be taken at what times is important for the present and future wellbeing of young people.
>
> *Wade et al., 2005:192*

In order that it is sufficiently flexible to address the main possible outcomes, which range from a grant of refugee status with leave to remain to refusal of asylum (see pages 28–29), the guidance suggests planning should incorporate:

- a transitional plan for the duration of uncertainty regarding immigration status;
- a longer-term prospective plan for the young person's continued residence, if granted long-term permission to stay (five years), which (although there is not a guarantee of further leave to remain, there is a strong likelihood of long-term residence in the UK) should be the primary focus of the pathway plan;
- a return to their country of origin whether that happens because the young person decides to leave the UK, or he is required to do so.

Financial support for UASCs

Whilst local authorities can claim a Home Office grant for all UASCs that they are looking after, the grant for care-leaving UASCs is targeted at those authorities with the highest numbers. Local authorities with more than 25 UASCs in full-time education can claim a grant from the Home Office (£150 per week 2013/2014) for each additional UASC care leaver in full-time education.

Guidance (DfE, 2010b)

This applies whether or not the authority is in receipt of a Home Office grant. Financial support for looked after UASCs should reflect their needs as looked after young people (eligible care leavers) and their immigration needs. Financial policies should highlight their entitlements and how their immigration status may impact on current and future entitlements.

Pathway plans should:

- address funding arrangements for education and training and how a young person's immigration status may limit education, training and employment opportunities;
- always consider the implications for the young people if their application to extend their leave to remain is refused, or their appeal against refusal of that application is dismissed. In such circumstances the person may become ineligible for further support and assistance because of the effect of Schedule 3 Nationality, Immigration and Asylum Act 2002 (DfE, 2010b:6.28–30).

Black and minority ethnic young people

As Stein (2009a) suggests, black and minority ethnic young people face many similar challenges to other young people leaving care. In addition they may experience racial discrimination and identity problems arising from a lack of knowledge or contact with family and community. Despite this, they are not identified in the guidance as requiring additional specialist support.

Care leavers in the youth justice system

Local authorities' care-leaving policies are required to include a comprehensive response to care leavers who are involved with the criminal justice services and/or are in custody:

> This requires the establishment of effective working relationships between the leaving care service and local criminal justice services, especially the youth offending team. This will help ensure that in each individual case, the right links are made between pathway planning and plans to divert young people from offending, to support them in custody or to supervise them in the community on release from custody.
>
> *DfE, 2010b:6.33*

Further reading

Websites: a range of useful and up-to-date information and advice is available from: www.leavingcare.org; www.childrenslegalcentre.com; and www.voiceyp.org.

Wheal, A (ed.) (2005) *The Care Leaving Handbook* provides perspectives on a range of leaving-care issues. For up-to-date information, these should be followed up on the above websites.

USEFUL WEBSITES

www.childrenslegalcentre.com
Coram Children's Legal Centre provides free legal information, advice and representation to children, young people, their families, carers and professionals, as well as international consultancy on child law and children's rights.

www.coram.org.uk
Coram is a charity committed to improving the lives of the UK's most vulnerable children and young people.

www.leavingcare.org
The website of the National Care Advisory Service (NCAS), the leading national body aiming to improve policy and practice relating to young people's transition from care to adulthood. Its aims include seeing that all care leavers are able to achieve their full potential and aspirations.

www.lgo.org.uk
The LGO's online bulletin *C&YP* (first issue October 2013) publishes details of a range of complaints by children and young people, many featuring local authorities' responses to children looked after or who whom the local authority failed to protect.

www.nairo.org.uk
The NAIRO website is a useful source of commentary on developments and current concerns for the service.

www.privatefostering.org.uk
Somebody Else's Child is a well-designed informative website hosted by BAAF.

www.voiceyp.org
Coram Voice is a charity committed to getting young voices heard, designed for young people in care or living away from home

www.yjbpublications.justice.gov.uk
The Youth Justice Board publishes a range of informative literature covering recent developments in the treatment of young offenders. Many are free to download.

GLOSSARY

Advocate
A person, independent of the local authority who articulates what a child (or adult) says that they want to happen, or not to happen.

Arrest
The apprehension of a person suspected of criminal activities.

CAFCASS
Child and Family Court Advisory and Support Service, see ss 11–17 Criminal Justice and Court Services Act 2000.

Care proceedings
Family court proceedings (s. 31 Children Act 1989) to seek orders for the protection of children suffering or at risk of suffering significant harm.

Child
A person under the age of 18 (s. 105 Children Act 1989).

Child of the family
A technical description defined in s. 105(1) Children Act 1989.

Children's guardian
A person, usually employed by CAFCASS, who independently advises the court and represents the interests of children in care and other public law proceedings.

Civil partnership
A formal legal status under the Civil Partnership Act 2004, entered into by same-sex couples.

Foster care
An arrangement made by a local authority for a child to live with a foster carer.

Guardian
A person appointed to assume parental responsibility for an orphaned child either by a deceased parent or by a court (s. 5 Children Act 1989).

Inherent jurisdiction
The historic power of the High Court to make orders to safeguard the welfare of adults or children where there is a gap in statutory provision.

Legislation
Acts of Parliament, also referred to as statutes.

Mental capacity
The capacity to make a decision at the time it needs to be made.

Obiter or obiter dicta (something said in passing)
Remarks made in a judgment or opinion that may helpfully elaborate or explain the decision reached by the court but are not legally significant.

Parental responsibility
A technical term covering all the legal powers and duties of parents. It is only held by parents, guardians and those with the benefit of certain orders and agreements under ss 4, 4A, 8, 12, 14A–G and 33 Children Act 1989 and ss 25 and 46 Adoption and Children Act 2002.

Private fostering
A fostering arrangement made privately without the involvement of the local authority.

Private law
That part of the law regulating arrangements between individuals.

Public law
That part of the law regulating arrangements between individuals and the state.

Relative
Grandparent, brother, sister, uncle or aunt (whether of the full blood or half blood or by affinity) or step-parent.

Secure accommodation
Accommodation provided for the purposes of restricting liberty.

Special guardianship
A legal status between residence and adoption under s. 14A–G Children Act 1989.

Step-parent
A person married to a birth parent of a child.

Wardship
The jurisdiction of the High Court to make a child a ward of court and assume responsibility for her welfare.

BIBLIOGRAPHY

All Party Parliamentary Group (2012) *Inquiry into Children Missing from Care* (London: DfE)

Bainham, A (2005) *Children: The Modern Law* 3rd edn (Bristol: Family Law)

Bainham, A (2013) 'Public and private children law: an under-explored relationship' 25(2) *Child and Family Law Quarterly* 138

Bainham, A and S Gilmore (2013) *Children the Modern Law* 4th edn (Bristol: Family Law)

Baker, C (2006) 'Disabled children's experience of permanency in the looked after system' 37(7) *British Journal of Social Work* 1173–88

Ball, C (1990) 'The Children Act 1989: origins, aims and current concerns' in P Carter, T Jeffs and M Smith (eds) *Social Work and Social Welfare Year Book 2* (Milton Keynes: Open University Press)

Ball, C (1998) 'Regulating child care: from the Children Act 1948 to the present day' 3 *Child and Family Social Work* 163–71

Ball, C (2003) 'The changed nature of adoption: a challenge for the legislators' in G Miller (ed.) *Frontiers of Family Law* (Aldershot: Ashgate)

Berridge, D (2008) *Educating Difficult Adolescents: Effective Education for Children in Care with Behavioural and Emotional Difficulties* (London: Jessica Kingsley)

Biehal, N, J Clayden, M Stein and J Wade (1995) *Moving On: Young People and Leaving Care Schemes* (London: HMSO)

Biswas, P, P Corina and C Mouser (2010) *Young Views and Voices: A Report on Young Service Users' Perspectives on Safeguarding* www.nscb.norfolk.gov.uk/documents

Bridge, C (2012) 'Case note: *Coventry City Council v C, B, CA and CH* [2012]' (November) *Family Law* 1255

British Association for Adoption and Fostering www.privatefostering.org.uk

Chase, E, A Simon and S Jackson (2006) *In Care and After: A Positive Perspective* (London: Routledge)

Chief Secretary to the Treasury (2003) *Every Child Matters* Cm 5860 (London: TSO)

Children's Rights Director for England (2009) *Planning, Placement and Review: A Report of a Children's Consultation to the DCSF* (London: DCSF)

Clough, R, R Bullock and A Ward (2006) *What Works in Residential Child Care* (London: NCB)

Coram Children's Legal Centre (2013) *Happy Birthday? Disputing the Age of Children in the Immigration System* Executive Summary (Colchester: University of Essex/Coram Children's Legal Centre)

Davies, C and H Ward (2012) *Safeguarding Children Across Services: Messages from Research* (London: Jessica Kingsley)

Department for Children, Schools and Families (2008) *Children Act 1989 Guidance and Regulations Volume 1: Court Orders* (Nottingham: DCSF)

Department for Children, Schools and Families (2010a) *Working Together to Safeguard Children* (Nottingham: DCSF)

Department for Children, Schools and Families (2010b) *Sufficiency: Statutory Guidance on Securing Sufficient Accommodation for Looked After Children* (London: DCSF)

Department for Children, Schools and Families (2010c) *IRO Handbook: Statutory Guidance for Independent Reviewing Officers and Local Authorities on their Functions in Relation to Case Management and Review for Looked After Children* (Nottingham: DCSF)

Department for Children, Schools and Families and Department for Communities and Local Government (2008) *Provision of Accommodation for 16 and 17 Year Olds Who May Be Homeless and/or Require Accommodation* (Nottingham: DCSF)

Department for Children, Schools and Families and Department of Health (2009) *Promoting the Health and Wellbeing of Looked After Children* (Nottingham: DCSF)

Department for Constitutional Affairs (2007) *Mental Capacity Act 2005: Code of Practice* (London: TSO)

Department for Education (2010a) *Family and Friends Care: Statutory Guidance for Local Authorities* (London: DfE)

Department for Education (2010b) *Guidance and Regulations Volume 3: Planning Transition to Adulthood for Care Leavers* (London: DfE)

Department for Education (2011a) *Guidance and Regulations Volume 4: Fostering Services* (London: DfE)

Department for Education (2011b) *Children Act 1989 Guidance and Regulations Volume 5: Children's Homes* (London: DfE)

Department for Education (2011c) *The Munro Review of Child Protection: Final Report: A Child Centred System* Cm 8062 (London: DfE)

Department for Education (2011d) *Fostering Services: National Minimum Standards* (London: DfE)

Department for Education (2013a) *Call for Views: Adoption Contact Arrangements and Sibling Placements – Summary of Feedback and Government Responses* (London: DfE)

Department for Education (2013b) *Children's Homes Data Pack* (London: DfE)

Department for Education (2013c) *Improving Permanence for Looked After Children* (London: DfE)

Department for Education (2013d) *Delegation of Authority: Amendments to the Children Act 1989 Regulations and Guidance* (London: DfE)

Department for Education (2013e) *Children Looked After in England (Including Adoption and Care Leavers) Year Ending March 2013* (London: DfE) www.gov.uk/government/publications/children-looked-after-in-england-including-adoption

Department for Education (2013f) *Statutory Guidance on Children Who Run Away or Go Missing from Home or Care* (London: DfE)

Department for Education and Skills (2003) *If This Were My Child ...: A Councillor's Guide to Being a Good Corporate Parent* (Nottingham: DfES)

Department for Education and Skills (2005a) *The Replacement Children Act 1989 Guidance on Private Fostering* (London: DfES)

Department for Education and Skills (2005b) *National Minimum Standards for Private Fostering* (London: DfES)

Department for Education and Skills (2006) *Care Matters: Transforming the Lives of Children and Young People in Care* Cm 6932 (London: DfES)

Department for Education and Skills (2007) *Care Matters: Time for Change* Cm 7137 (London: DfES)

Department for Education and Skills and Others (2006) *Future Positive: A Resource Guide for People Working with Disabled Care Leavers* 2nd edn (London: DfES)

Department of Health (1998) *Caring for Children Away from Home: Messages from Research* (London: Wiley)

Department of Health (2000) *Adoption: A New Approach* (London: DH)

Department of Health (2002) *Promoting the Health of Looked After Children* (London: DH)

Department of Health, Department for Education and Employment and Home Office (2000) *Framework for the Assessment of Children in Need and their Families* (London: TSO)

Department of Health and Social Security (1985) *Social Work Decisions in Child Care: Recent Research Findings and their Implications* (London: DHSS)

Family Justice Review Panel (2011) *Family Justice Review* (London: Ministry of Justice, DfE and Welsh Government)

Farmer, E and E Lutman (2013) 'What contributes to outcomes for neglected children who are reunified with their parents? Findings from a five-year follow-up study' 29 *British Journal of Social Work* 559–78

Farmer E and S Moyers (2008) *Kinship Care: Fostering Effective Family and Friends Placements* (London: Jessica Kingsley)

Fletcher, B (1993) *Not Just a Name: The Views of Young People in Foster and Residential Care* (London: London Consumer Council)

Fortin, J (2001) 'Children's rights and physical force' 13(3) *Child and Family Law Quarterly* 243

Fortin, J (2009) *Children's Rights and the Developing Law* 3rd edn (Cambridge: Cambridge University Press)

Fortin, J (2011) 'A decade of the HRA and its impact on children's rights' *Family Law* 179

George, V (1970) *Foster Care* (London: Routledge & Keegan Paul)

Golding, K (2010) 'Multi-agency and specialist working to meet the mental health needs of children in care and adopted' 15(4) *Clinical Child Psychology and Psychiatry* 573–87

Green, H, A McGinnity, H Meltzer, T Ford and R Goodman (2005) *Mental Health of Children and Young People in Great Britain 2004: A Survey by the Office for National Statistics* (Basingstoke: Palgrave Macmillan)

Griffith, J A (1966) *Central Departments and Local Authorities* (London: Allen & Unwin)

Harker, R, D Dobel, D Berridge and R Sinclair (2004) *Taking Care of Education: An Evaluation of the Education of Looked After Children* (London: NCB)

Hart, D and A Williams (2013) *Putting Corporate Parenting into Practice: A Handbook for Councillors* 2nd edn (London: NCB)

Hayden, C (2005) 'More than a Piece of Paper? Personal Education Plans and Looked After Children in England' 10 *Child and Family Social Work* 343–52

Hendrick, H (1994) *Child Welfare in England 1872–1989* (London: Routledge)

Holt, K (2014) *Child Protection* (Basingstoke: Palgrave Macmillan)

HM Government (2007) *Statutory Guidance on Making Arrangements to Safeguard and Promote the Welfare of Children under Section 11 of the Children Act 2004* (London: DfES)

HM Government (2010) *The Children Act 1989 Guidance and Regulations Volume 2: Care Planning, Placement and Case Review* (Nottingham: HM Government)

HM Government (2013) *Working Together to Safeguard Children: A Guide to Inter-agency Working to Safeguard and Promote the Welfare of Children* (London: HM Government)

Hollingworth, K E (2012) 'Participation in social, leisure and informal learning activities among care leavers in England: positive outcomes for educational participation' 17 *Child and Family Social Work* 438–47

Holman, R (1973) *Trading in Children: A Study of Private Fostering* (London: Routledge & Keegan Paul)

Home Office (1960) *Report of the Committee on Children and Young Persons*, Cmnd 1191 (London: HMSO)

Home Office UK Border Agency (2013) *Grant Instructions to Local Authorities Financial Year 2013/14* (London: Home Office)

House of Commons (1984) *Second Report from the Social Services Committee: Session 1983–1984 Volume 1* (London: HMSO)

House of Commons (1998) *Health Committee Second Report on Children Looked After by Local Authorities: Report and Proceedings of the Committee Volume 1* (London: HMSO)

Hunt, J (2009) 'Family and friends care' in G Schofield and J Simmonds (eds) *The Child Placement Handbook* (London: BAAF)

Jackson, S (ed.) (2001) *Nobody Ever Told Us School Mattered: Raising the Educational Attainments of Children in Care* (London: BAAF)

Jackson, S (ed.) (2013) *Pathways through Education for Young People in Care: Ideas from Research and Practice* (London: BAAF)

Jane Held Consulting Ltd (2006) *Qualitative Study: The Use by Local Authorities of Secure Children's Homes* Research Report RR 749 (London: DfES)

Knowles, G and M Sharp (2012) 'IRO service: still a work in progress?' (parts 1 and 2) *Family Law* (November) 1258 and (December) 1377

Lambert, L (1983) *A Study of the Health of Children in Care, Using Information Derived from the National Child Development Study* (London: NCB Report to the Social Science Research Council)

Laming, Lord (2003) *The Victoria Climbié Inquiry* Cm 5730 (London: DH and Home Department)

Laws, S, R Wilson and S Rabindrakumar (2012) *Concurrent Planning Study: Interim Report* (London: Coram) www.coram.org.uk

Levy, A and B Kahan (1991) *The Pindown Experience and the Protection of Children* (Stafford: Staffordshire County Council)

Local Government Association and National Children's Bureau (2012) *10 Questions to Ask if You Are Scrutinising Services for Looked After Children* (London: LGA)

Local Government Ombudsman (2013) *C&YP Issues* www.lgo.org.uk

Lord Chancellor's Department (1997) *Final Report of the Children Act Advisory Committee* (London: Lord Chancellor's Department)

MacDonald, A (2009) 'The caustic dichotomy: political vision and resourcing in the care system' 21(1) *Child and Family Law Quarterly* 30–46

Masson, J (1992) 'Managing risk under the Children Act 1989: diversion in child care' *Child Abuse Review* 103

Masson, J (2000) 'From Curtis to Waterhouse: state care and child protection in the UK 1945–2000' in N Sandford, J Katz, J Eekelaar and M Maclean (eds) *Cross Currents: Family Law and Policy in the US and England* (Oxford: Oxford University Press)

Masson, J (2005) 'Emergency intervention to protect children: using and avoiding legal controls' 17(1) *Child and Family Law Quarterly* 75

Meltzer, H, R Corbin, T Gatward, R Goodman and T Ford (2003) *The Mental Health of Young People Looked After by Local Authorities in England* (London: TSO)

Millham, S, R Bullock, K Hosie and M Little (1986) *Lost in Care: The Problem of Maintaining Links between Children in Care and their Families* (Aldershot: Gower)

Millham, S, R Bullock, K Hosie and M Little (1989) *Access Disputes in Child Care* (Gower: Aldershot)

Ministry of Health and Ministry of Education (1946) *Report of the Care of Children Committee* Cmd 6922 (London: HMSO)

Monkton, W (1945) *The Circumstances which Led to the Boarding Out of Denis and Terence O'Neill at Bank Farm, Minsterly and the Steps Taken to Supervise their Welfare* Cmd 6366 (London: HMSO)

Morgan, R (2005) *Getting the Best from Complaints: The Children's View* (Newcastle-upon-Tyne: Commission for Social Care Inspection)

Morgan, R (2006) *Placements, Decisions and Reviews: A Children's Views Report* (Newcastle upon Tyne: Commission for Social Care Inspection)

Murphy, J (2003) 'Children in need: the limits of local authority accountability' 23 *Legal Studies* 103

National Association of Independent Reviewing Officers www.nairo.org.uk

Ofsted (2013) *Missing Children* www.ofsted.gov.uk.resources/120364

Packman, J (1975) *The Child's Generation* (Oxford: Blackwell & Robertson)

Packman, J, J Randall and N Jacques (1986) *Who Needs Care?* (Oxford: Blackwell)

Parry, M (2000) 'Secure Accommodation: the Cinderella of family law' 2 *Child and Family Law Quarterly* 101

Philpot, T (2001) *A Very Private Practice: An Investigation into Private Fostering* (London: BAAF)

Pickford, J and P Dugmore (2012) *Youth Justice and Social Work* 2nd edn (London: Sage)

Pithouse, A and A Crowley (2007) 'Adults Rule? Children, Advocacy and Complaints to Social Services' 21 *Children and Society* 201

Pringle, M K (1965) *Deprivation and Education* (London: Longman)

Probert, R (2012) *Cretney and Probert's Family Law* 8th edn (London: Sweet & Maxwell)

Rao, P and A Ali (2010) 'Looked after and adopted children: how should specialist CAMHS be involved?' 34(2) *Adoption and Fostering* 58–72

Richardson, J (2002) *The Mental Health of Looked After Children: Bright Futures, Working with Vulnerable Young People* (London: Mental Health Foundation)

Schofield, G (2005) 'The voice of the child in family placement decision-making: a developmental model' 29(1) *Adoption and Fostering* 29–44

Schofield, G and M Beek (2005) 'Risk and resilience in long-term foster care' 35(8) *British Journal of Social Work* 1283–301

Schofield, G and J Simmonds (eds) (2009) *The Child Placement Handbook* (London: BAAF)

Schofield, G, J Thoburn, D Howell and J Dickens (2007) 'The search for stability and permanence: modelling the pathways of long-stay looked after children' 37 *British Journal of Social Work* 619–42

Sempik, J, H Ward and I Darker (2008) 'Emotional and behavioural difficulties of young people at entry into care' 13(2) *Clinical Child Psychology and Psychiatry* 221–33

Simmonds, J (2011) *The Role of Special Guardianship in Permanency Planning for Children in England and Wales* (London: BAAF)

Sinclair, I (2005) *Fostering Now: Messages from Research* (London: Jessica Kingsley)

Sinclair, I, C Baker, J Lee and I Gibbs (2007) *The Pursuit of Permanence: A Study of the English Child Care System* (London: Jessica Kingsley)

Sinclair, I, K Wilson and I Gibbs (2005) *Foster Placements: Why They Succeed and Why They Fail* (London: Jessica Kingsley)

Social Exclusion Unit (2003) *A Better Education for Children in Care: The Issues* (London: Cabinet Office)

Stather, J (2013) *Secure Accommodation Handbook* (Bristol: Family Law)

Stein, M (2004) *What Works for Young People Leaving Care?* (Barkingside: Barnardo's)

Stein, M (2009a) *Quality Matters in Children's Services: Messages from Research* (London: Jessica Kingsley)

Stein, M (2009b) 'Young people leaving care' in G Schofield and J Simmonds (eds) *The Child Placement Handbook* (London: BAAF)

Thoburn, J (2003) 'The risks and rewards of adoption for children in the public care' 15(4) *Child and Family Law Quarterly* 391

Timms, J and J Thoburn (2006) 'Your shout! Looked after children's perspectives on the Children Act 1989' 28(2) *Journal of Social Welfare and Family Law* 153–70

Thomas, N (2009) 'Listening to Children and Young People' in G Schofield and J Simmonds (eds) *The Child Placement Handbook* (London: BAAF)

Thomas, N (2011) 'Care planning and review for looked after children: fifteen years of slow progress?' 41 *British Journal of Social Work* 387–98

Utting, W (1997) *People Like Us: The Report of the Review of the Safeguards for Children Living Away from Home* (London: TSO)

Voice for the Child in Care (2004) *Start with the Child, Stay with the Child: A Blueprint for a Child-Centred Approach to Children and Young People in Public Care* (London: Voice for the Child in Care)

Wade, J and J Dixon (2006) 'Making a home, finding a job: investigating early housing and employment outcomes for young people leaving care' 11(3) *Child and Family Social Work* 199–208

Wade, J, F Mitchell and G Baylis (2005) *Unaccompanied Asylum Seeking Children: The Response of Social Work Services* (London: BAAF)

Waterhouse, R (2000) *Lost in Care: Report of the Tribunal of Inquiry into the Abuse of Children in Care in the Former County Council Areas of Gwynedd and Clwyd since 1974* (London: TSO)

Westwood, J (2014) *Children in Need of Support* (Basingstoke: Palgrave Macmillan)

Wheal, A (ed.) (2005) *The Leaving Care Handbook* (Lyme Regis: Russell House)

White, R, P Carr and N Lowe (2008) *The Children Act in Practice* 4th edn (London: Butterworths)

Wright, F (2012) 'Social work practice with unaccompanied asylum-seeking children facing removal' *British Journal of Social Work* 1–18

United Nations Committee on the Rights of the Child (2005) *CRC General Comment No 6* www.unhcr.org/refworld/docid/42dd174b4.html

INDEX